P9-CFJ-161

Chicago Public Library
C
P
L
REFERENCE

Volume 5
PLANTS

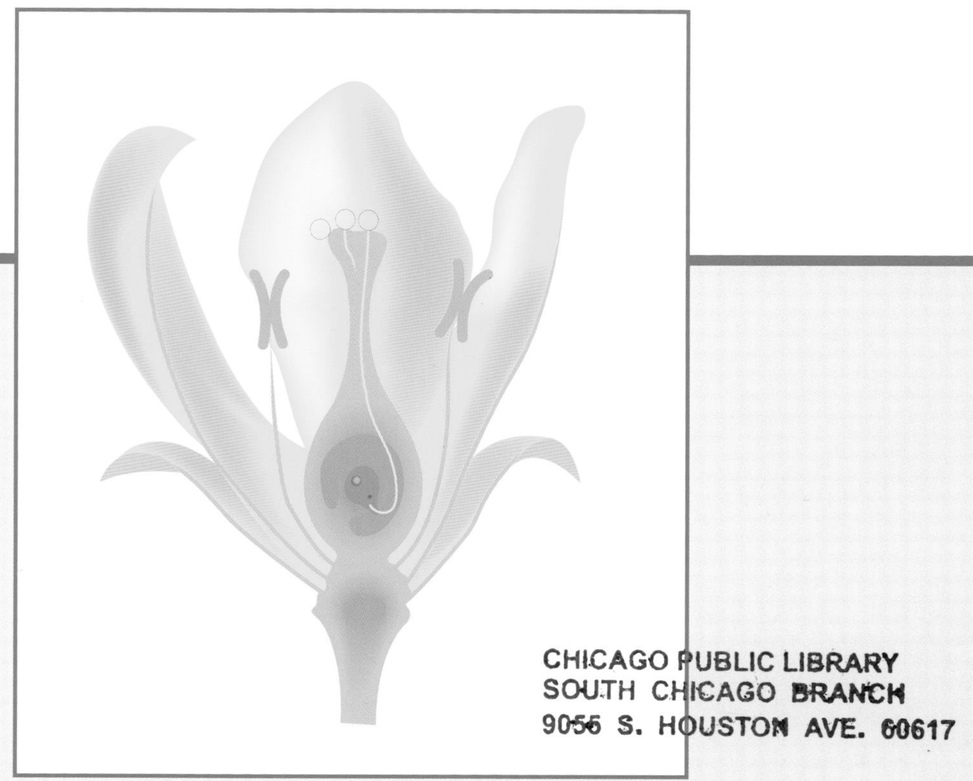

GROLIER

Published 2004 by Grolier
An imprint of Scholastic Library Publishing
Old Sherman Turnpike
Danbury, Connecticut 06816

FOR THE BROWN REFERENCE GROUP plc

Contributors:	Amy-Jane Beer, Ph.D., Ian Crofton, David and Margaret Evans, Andrew Lack
Consultant:	Nick Turland Assistant Curator Missouri Botanical Garden
Project Editor:	Anne Wanjie
Deputy Editor:	Jim Martin
Development Editor:	Richard Beatty
Copy Editors:	Lesley Campbell-Wright John Jackson
Designer:	Joan Curtis
Picture Researcher:	Becky Cox
Illustrators:	Darren Awuah, Richard Burgess, Mark Walker
Indexer:	Kay Ollerenshaw
Managing Editor:	Bridget Giles
Design Manager:	Lynne Ross
Production Director:	Alastair Gourlay
Editorial Director:	Lindsey Lowe

Printed and bound in Hong Kong

ABOUT THIS SET

What could be more fascinating than the story of life? It is all told in *Biology Matters!* Across ten topical volumes this set reviews all fundamental life-science concepts. Each volume carefully introduces its topic, briefly examines the history, and fully displays all aspects of modern thinking about biology, ecology, evolution, genetics, cell biology, microbiology, life forms from every kingdom, and the human body. The clear text explains complex concepts and terms in full. Hundreds of photographs, artworks, and "Closeup" boxes provide details on key aspects. Simple, safe experiments encourage readers to explore biology in "Try This" boxes. "What Do You Think?" panels pose questions that test the reader's comprehension. "Applications" boxes show how biological knowledge enhances daily life and technology, while "Red Herring" boxes outline failed theories. "Hot Debate" panels illuminate the disagreements and discussions that rage in the biological sciences, and "Genetic Perspective" boxes outline the latest genetic research.

Volume ISBN 0-7172-5984-6
Set ISBN 0-7172-5979-X

Library of Congress Cataloging-in-Publication Data

Biology Matters!
p. cm.
Contents: v.1. Introduction to biology—v.2. Cell biology—v.3. Genetics—v.4. Microorganisms—v.5. Plants—v.6. Animals—v.7. The human body—v.8. Reproduction—v.9. Evolution—v.10. Ecology.
ISBN 0-7172-5979-X (set : alk.paper)—ISBN 0-7172-5980-3 (v.1 : alk. paper)—ISBN 0-7172-5981-1 (v.2 : alk. paper)—ISBN 0-7172-5982-X (v.3 : alk. paper)—ISBN 0-7172-5983-8 (v.4 : alk. paper)—ISBN 0-7172-5984-6 (v.5 : alk. paper)—ISBN 0-7172-5985-4 (v.6 : alk. paper)—ISBN 0-7172-5986-2 (v.7 : alk. paper)—ISBN 0-7172-5987-0 (v.8 : alk. paper)—ISBN 0-7172-5988-9 (v.9 : alk. paper)—ISBN 0-7172-5989-7 (v.10 : alk. paper)
1. Biology—Juvenile literature. [1. Biology.] I. Grolier Publishing Company

QH309.2.B56 2004
507—dc22

2003056942

PICTURE CREDITS (b=bottom; t=top)
Front Cover: Oxford Scientific Films: Joe McDonald.
Ardea: Ian Beames 16, Liz Bomford 4, Piers Cavendish 55, John Clegg 36, 58b, Jean-Paul Ferrero 17, 53, Kenneth W. Fink 20, Francois Gohier 15, Steve Hopkin 52b, C. Knights 66b, J. M. Labat 11b, John Mason 54b, P. Morris 19b, 58t, A. P. Peterson 43b, Peter Steyn 5, Alan Weaving 50b, Jim Zipp 51r; **ARS:** 30t, 46; **Bridgeman:** Archives Charmet 45; **The Brown Reference Group plc:** 51l, 64; **Bruce Coleman:** Anders Blomquist 19t, Colin Varndell 32; **Corbis:** David Aubrey 24, Owen Franken 31, Philip Gould 44, Farrell Grehan 42b, Wolfgang Kaehler 11t, Bob Krist 52t, Bill Ross 27, Lee Snider 57; **Getty Images:** Julie Toy 70; **Nature Photo Library:** Alfo 38, Jose B. Ruiz 8; **NHPA:** A.N.T 69, B. & C. Alexander 14, Laurie Campbell 23t, E. A. James 13, Norbert Wu 66t; **NOAA:** 61, David Sinson 67; **Oxford Scientific Films:** 37t, 37b, Bob Gibbons 33, Lawrence Gould 63, Karen Gowlett-Holmes 62, C. E. Jeffree 11c, Breck P. Kent 38t, Joe McDonald/ AA 23b, Stan Olsolinski 21, Peter Ryley 49, Sue Scott 59, Nigel Westwood/ SAL 54t, David Wrigglesworth 43t; **Photodisc:** 38b; **Science Photo Library:** Chris Knapton 42t; **Topham:** 18, 28, Dinochia/Imageworks 56, Edy Purnomo/Imageworks 50t; **USDA:** Bill Tarpening 6; **Visuals Unlimited:** Sylvan Wittwer 30b.

Volume 5
Plants

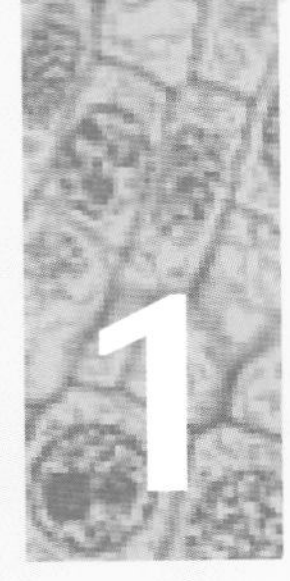

1 What Is a Plant?

Plants form one of the five kingdoms of living things. Plants include ferns that produce spores, cone-bearing conifers, and plants that produce seeds using flowers.

There are hundreds of thousands of different species of plants on Earth. Plants vary from liverworts just a fraction of an inch high to giant redwood trees hundreds of feet tall.

▼ *Sunlight shines through pine trees. The trees use energy from the sun in the process of photosynthesis.*

The lives of plants

Plants make their own food by collecting energy from sunlight and using it to turn carbon dioxide and water into sugars. This process is called photosynthesis (see 7–12).

Plants are not the only organisms that make food by photosynthesis. Algae also photosynthesize. Organisms that photosynthesize have chloroplasts in their cells (see 7–8). Plant cells not only contain chloroplasts but differ from other organisms in one other important but not very obvious way. Plants cells have a cell wall made of a tough substance called cellulose. The only multicellular organisms other than plants to have a cell wall are fungi (see **1**: 21). Fungi are not plants: They cannot photosynthesize, and their cell walls are made out of a material called chitin.

Scientists think that the first land plants appeared about 500 million years ago. Bryophytes (liverworts, hornworts, and mosses) are similar to these first plants. Around 16,000 bryophyte species occur today. Unlike other plants, they do not have vascular tissues (structures that carry fluids around the plant). Bryophytes, ferns, and horsetails reproduce using spores (see **8**: 8–15).

Flowering plants are the biggest and most varied of all the plant divisions (major groups). They appeared more than 100 million years ago. Flowering plants mostly reproduce using seeds, and some have large flowers. The flowers attract insects and birds that feed on nectar (a sweet liquid) from the plant. While visiting flowers, insects carry pollen (which contains male sex cells) from one plant to another. Male sex cells fertilize the plants. Other flowering plants, including many broadleaved trees and grasses, have small, insignificant-looking flowers. These plants spread their pollen on the wind.

▼ *Seaweeds can be green, red, or brown. Since they need a place to attach to with access to sunlight, seaweeds generally live in shallow, coastal areas.*

WHAT ARE ALGAE?

Algae are most familiar from wet environments: The slime on wet rocks and the green color in rivers, lakes, and seawater are caused by millions of tiny algae. There are thousands of species. Many algae are single-celled organisms, but seaweeds are multicellular algae. From the outside seaweeds look like plants, but they have no roots, and their stems do not contain tubes that transport water and food.

Scientists once classified algae as types of plants but now think the situation is more complex. Some classify green algae with plants, but others put them with protists (see **4**: 20–31). Seaweeds, too, can be classified as plants or protists. Most scientists have renamed blue-green algae as cyanobacteria and placed them with bacteria.

2 How Plants Work

Plants are vital to life on Earth because of their ability to make food. They use their leaves, stems, and roots in the process.

Herbivores are animals that eat plants. They get their energy from digesting the plants and so take the energy the plants captured through photosynthesis. Predators (hunters) then eat the herbivores. In aquatic (watery) environments seaweeds (see 58–70) and tiny single-celled algae (see **4**: 20–31 and **10**: 40–49) are more usually the base of food chains and webs.

Plants are the basis of all life on land (see **10**: 5). Plants photosynthesize, using sunlight energy to make their own food and build their tissues. Sunlight, carbon dioxide, water, and minerals from the soil, such as nitrogen and phosphorus, are all most plants need to grow.

▼ *Cows eating plants. Plants are producers: They form the base of all food chains on land. Animals are consumers: They eat plants, animals that eat plants, or other meat eaters.*

The plant body

Like animals, plants consist of many tiny cells (see **2**: 10–19). Plant and animal cells are similar, but plant cells have three unique features:

- They are surrounded by a tough cell wall made mainly of cellulose.

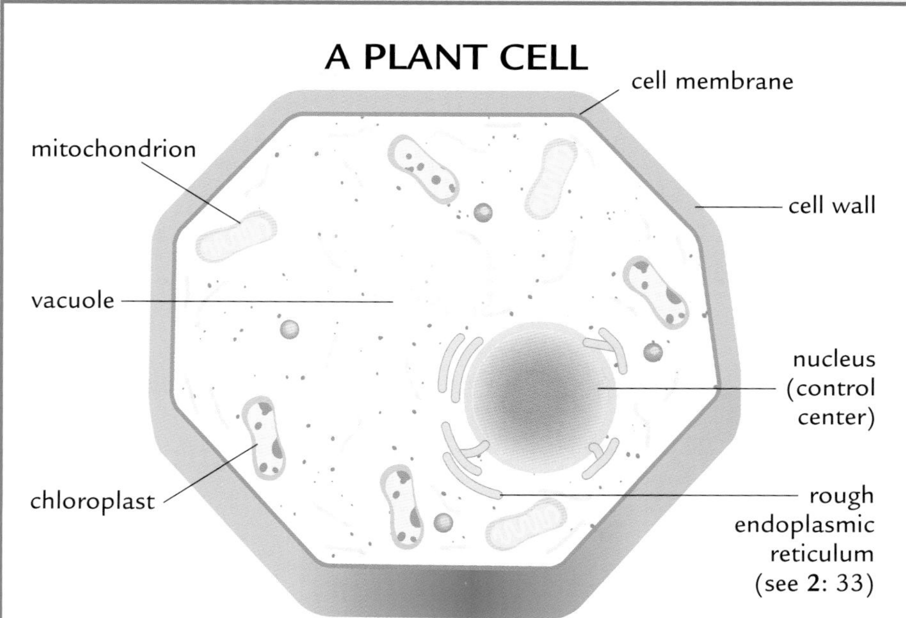

Plant cells have structures called chloroplasts inside which photosynthesis takes place. Plant cells also have mitochondria, which produce energy through respiration (see 1: 35).

- They have one or more large saclike vacuoles. A vacuole is a storage space filled with a watery liquid called cell sap.
- Some plant cells have chloroplasts, which contain chlorophyll, a green chemical that enables photosynthesis to occur (see below).

Not all plant cells are the same, but the basic structure is similar in leaves, green

PHOTOSYNTHESIS

The basic chemical reaction of photosynthesis is:

carbon dioxide (CO_2) + **water** (H_2O) + **SUNLIGHT** → **glucose (a sugar)** ($C_6H_{12}O_6$) + **oxygen** (O_2)

This chemical reaction involves many steps. They include trapping energy from the sun, called the light reaction, and capturing carbon dioxide from the air, which does not need light and is called the dark reaction. Like animals, plants must respire to release energy for growth and cell function. Chemically this is photosynthesis in reverse: In the presence of oxygen glucose forms carbon dioxide and water. Photosynthesis is faster than respiration during the day. But at night respiration continues, and photosynthesis stops.

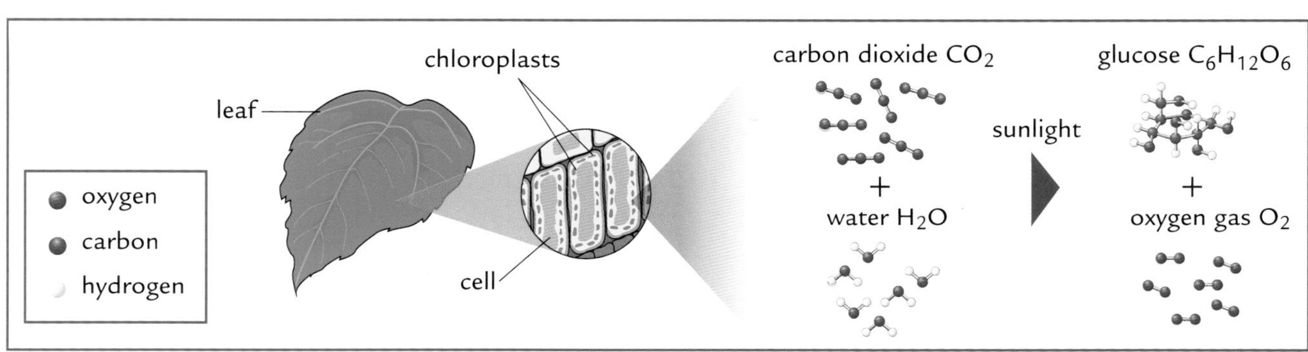

CHLOROPLASTS

Chloroplasts are organelles (miniorgans inside cells) that carry out photosynthesis in leaves and stems. There are usually many chloroplasts in each green cell. Pigments in the chloroplasts absorb energy-rich red light and reflect low-energy green light, which is why plants are green. The main green pigment is chlorophyll. A few plants do not have chloroplasts but feed on other plants as parasites.

The Maltese fungus (a plant, not a fungus) feeds on other plants as a parasite.

stems, and young roots. Minor differences occur in cells of flowers or fruits. These cells may be colored or enlarged. Some small cells have thick walls that form a skin, or epidermis. Only the green parts of the plant have cells with chloroplasts.

Cellulose is the most abundant of all naturally occurring organic, or carbon-containing,

TRANSPIRATION

Plants need water for:

- photosynthesis,
- transporting minerals and sugars inside the plant, and
- filling their cells to keep them rigid.

Plants lose water from their leaves through tiny holes called stomata. The water is evaporated (turned to gas) by heat from the sun. This process is called transpiration. As water evaporates through the stomata, more water is drawn up through the xylem (see **9**), like soda sucked through a straw. On a hot day a large tree can lose more than 22 gallons (100 liters) of water an hour through transpiration.

Transpiration is necessary for plants to draw water from their roots. Stomata also allow carbon dioxide-containing air into the cells for photosynthesis. Desert plants must reduce transpiration, or they dry out and die; but they still need stomata. Many desert plants have a thick and waxy waterproof cuticle (covering) on their stems or leaves. Some desert plants open their stomata only at night. They take carbon dioxide into their cells, dissolved as acid. During the day the plants use this carbon dioxide supply for photosynthesis.

compounds (see **1**: 28–30). Strengthening cells with thick cellulose walls gives flexible support. Leaf cells contain a lot of cellulose.

Cells in woody parts of plants have walls thickened with cellulose and also a tougher and more rigid substance called lignin. People use lignin fibers to make string and fabrics (see 52–53).

Moving water

Plants gather water and dissolved minerals through their roots and transport it to other parts of the plant. Most plants do this using elongated tubelike cells called xylem cells. Xylem cells are joined end to end and have lignin in the side walls for strength.

Some xylem cell walls taper or have large holes leading to the next xylem cell. Others lose their end walls altogether and form a continuous tube, or vessel, up the plant. Xylem tubes can be extremely long, going from the roots to the leaves of the tallest trees. Xylem cells grow like most other cells; but when they reach their full size, they die. Water and minerals still travel up the dead tubes. Lignin is tough and

TRANSPIRATION

Pull the stem of a plant through a hole in the center of a piece of card. Seal around the hole with petroleum jelly. Put the plant in a glass of water so the card rests on top. Cover it with a second glass, then leave it in sunlight. After 15 minutes you will see drops of water on the inverted glass.

WATCH THE WATER FLOW

Take a white cut flower such as a carnation, and put it into a container of blue dye, such as dilute ink. Watch the flower slowly turn blue as the plant takes up the colored water by transpiration. If you slice the stem up the middle and put the two sides into different colored dyes, the flower will end up with two different colors. That is because the xylem tubes do not connect to each other, so each section carries its own water supply.

LEAF STRUCTURE

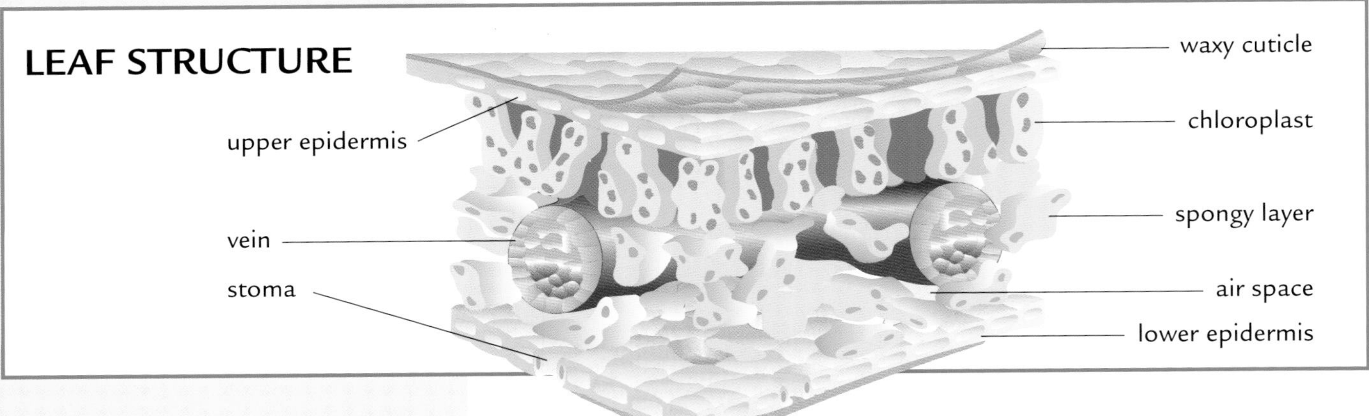

keeps the dead cells together after they die. Trees grow new xylem cells each year that form trunk rings (see **10:** 25). The old tubes continue to give support and form most of a tree's trunk.

HOT DEBATE

KEEPING A BALANCE

The oxygen in the air we breathe comes from photosynthesis. Photosynthesis takes carbon from carbon dioxide and produces oxygen as a byproduct (see 7). Before there was life on Earth, the atmosphere contained a lot of carbon dioxide but no oxygen. When photosynthesizing algae and plants evolved, the amount of oxygen in the atmosphere increased slowly to its present level of about 21 percent, and carbon dioxide decreased to 0.03 percent. The ratio is ideal for life, but what keeps the levels constant? One idea is that the whole world acts like a living organism to keep itself alive (see **10**: 65).

Coal, oil, and gas are fossilized plant remains. Burning fossil fuels releases carbon dioxide that the fossil plants originally took from the atmosphere when they grew. After years of people burning fossil fuels the level of carbon in the atmosphere has risen to 0.04 percent. That sounds small, but it is a 30 percent increase. Is it changing the balance? Can photosynthesis keep pace?

Moving sugars

Plants make sugars by photosynthesis. They transport the sugars to where they are needed, such as growing points or storage organs. Just as water flows through the xylem, dissolved sugars from photosynthesis also travel in tubes. The tubes that contain food are called phloem tubes. There are two types of phloem cells. Sieve elements are the cells in which movement of sugars takes place. These elements form a tube up the plant with perforations in the end walls. Beside the sieve elements are smaller companion cells. They connect to the sieve tubes and supply the energy for phloem transport. Water travels up the xylem by transpiration without using energy from the plant. However, the plant does use energy to make food flow through the phloem.

Leaves

Most photosynthesis occurs in leaves. Leaves vary in their shape and size from a 0.04 inch (1mm) duckweed leaf to a palm leaf 30 feet (10m) long. Most leaves expose a flat surface to the sun. The main leaf cells are green because they are full of chloroplasts. The long photosynthesizing cells are densely packed near the upper surface, with rounder cells loosely packed below.

Leaves have an epidermis (skin) of small cells on both surfaces, covered with a waxy cuticle that prevents too much water loss. The cuticle keeps gases such as carbon dioxide from entering or leaving. The lower epidermis, or sometimes both sides, has holes called stomata (singular: stoma). Gases are exchanged and water lost through these holes. The stomata open and shut depending on the concentration of carbon dioxide and water, and the time of day. Veins of xylem and phloem run through the leaves to supply water and take away sugars.

Not all plants have recognizable leaves. In hot places thin, spinelike leaves reduce transpiration. The spines of cacti are leaves, and one of their roles is defense. Some

▲ *The leaves of a banana plant can grow up to 10 feet (3m) long. In contrast, the inset photo shows duckweed, a plant with tiny leaves. It is the smallest flowering plant.*

▶ *The pincushion cactus has spiny leaves. They keep water loss by transpiration to a minimum in the hot surroundings.*

PLANTS AGAINST POLLUTION

Some plants absorb and store metals or other substances that are poisonous to animals. If they are planted near an old mine, the plants can clean up the area by rapid transpiration, accumulating the poisons and cleaning up the pollution.

In offices plants can be beneficial since they absorb pollutants such as vapors from inks and adhesives into their leaves. From there the chemicals go down to the roots, where bacteria break them down into less harmful chemicals.

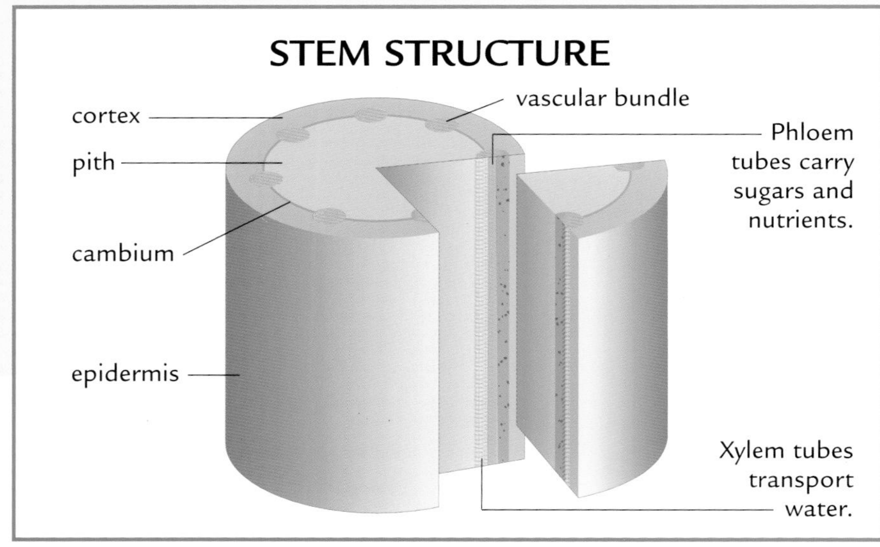

▲ *Plant stems support the leaves. Tubes inside the stems carry water and sugars to and from the leaves.*

plants have no leaves at all. In these plants photosynthesis happens mainly in the stems.

Stems

The stem of a new shoot is normally green. Like leaves, the stem carries out photosynthesis, but that is just one function of the stem. The main roles of stems are the transportation of water and sugars to and from the leaves, and supporting the plant.

Inside the skinlike epidermis is a green area called the cortex. It is where photosynthesis takes place. The cortex also covers and shields the phloem and xylem tubes. Stems develop a dividing layer of cells near the outside called the cambium. The cambium layer separates the outer phloem from the xylem nearer the center of the stem.

Trees and bushes become woody, and their stems can live for many years. Woody stems have another cambium outside the phloem. This area of cambium produces waxy waterproof cells on its outside that become the cork. The cork and the older phloem cells just underneath it together make the bark. Bark

▼ *A mature tree trunk is covered by bark. New xylem and phloem cells are produced by the cambium.*

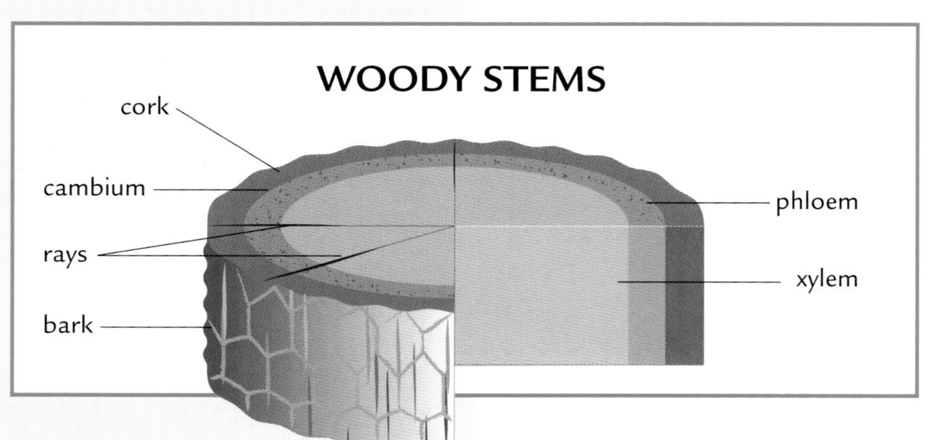

gets rubbed off but is replaced constantly by new layers of cambium and phloem cells.

After some years a mature tree trunk consists mainly of nonfunctional xylem cells with a thin layer of functional xylem and phloem cells around the outside, covered by the bark. Rings on tree trunks can be used to find out the age of the tree (see **10**: 25).

Roots

Roots anchor the plant and absorb water and minerals from the soil. Cell division occurs in the root cap, which also protects the root as it grows. The central xylem and phloem are surrounded by an endodermis. All the water that enters the root must pass through the endodermis cells, rather than the walls, so they act as a filter. There are root hairs on the outside of most young roots, making a greater surface area to better absorb water. Tree roots gradually become broader and woody in the same way as stems do.

Most plants live in partnership with fungi. The fungi live partly in the root cells but are connected with strings of cells in the soil. Fungi absorb water and minerals from the soil and exchange them with sugars from the plant.

◀ *The ancient woody roots of a beech tree spread out over a large distance around its base.*

ROOT STRUCTURE

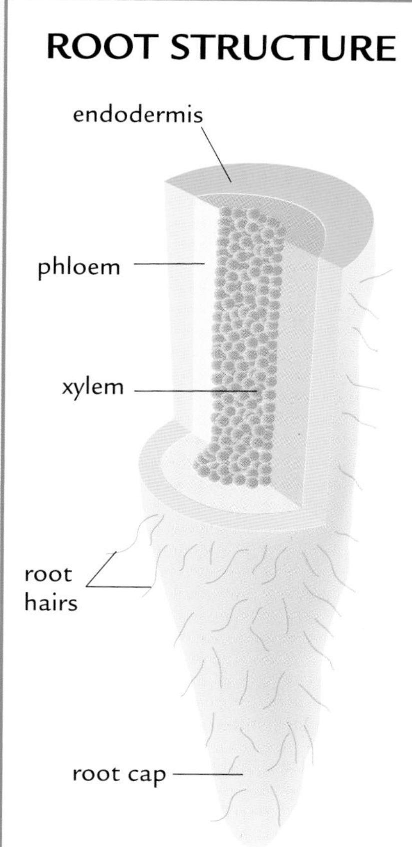

Roots anchor plants into the soil as well as absorbing water and minerals. In plants like carrots and turnips the roots store food.

3 Plant Adaptations

Nearly everywhere you go in the world, from the tropics to the polar regions, from dry, scorching deserts to the high slopes of the great mountain ranges, you will find plants growing.

Plants have evolved an enormous variety of forms and have adapted themselves to almost every land habitat in the world. Even hot geysers and frozen permanent snowfields provide a home for certain plantlike algae. Only near the North and South Poles, on very high mountain tops, in the ocean depths, and in the driest deserts are plants absent.

▼ *Even in the freezing conditions in tundra regions of the Canadian arctic purple saxifrage can grow through snow.*

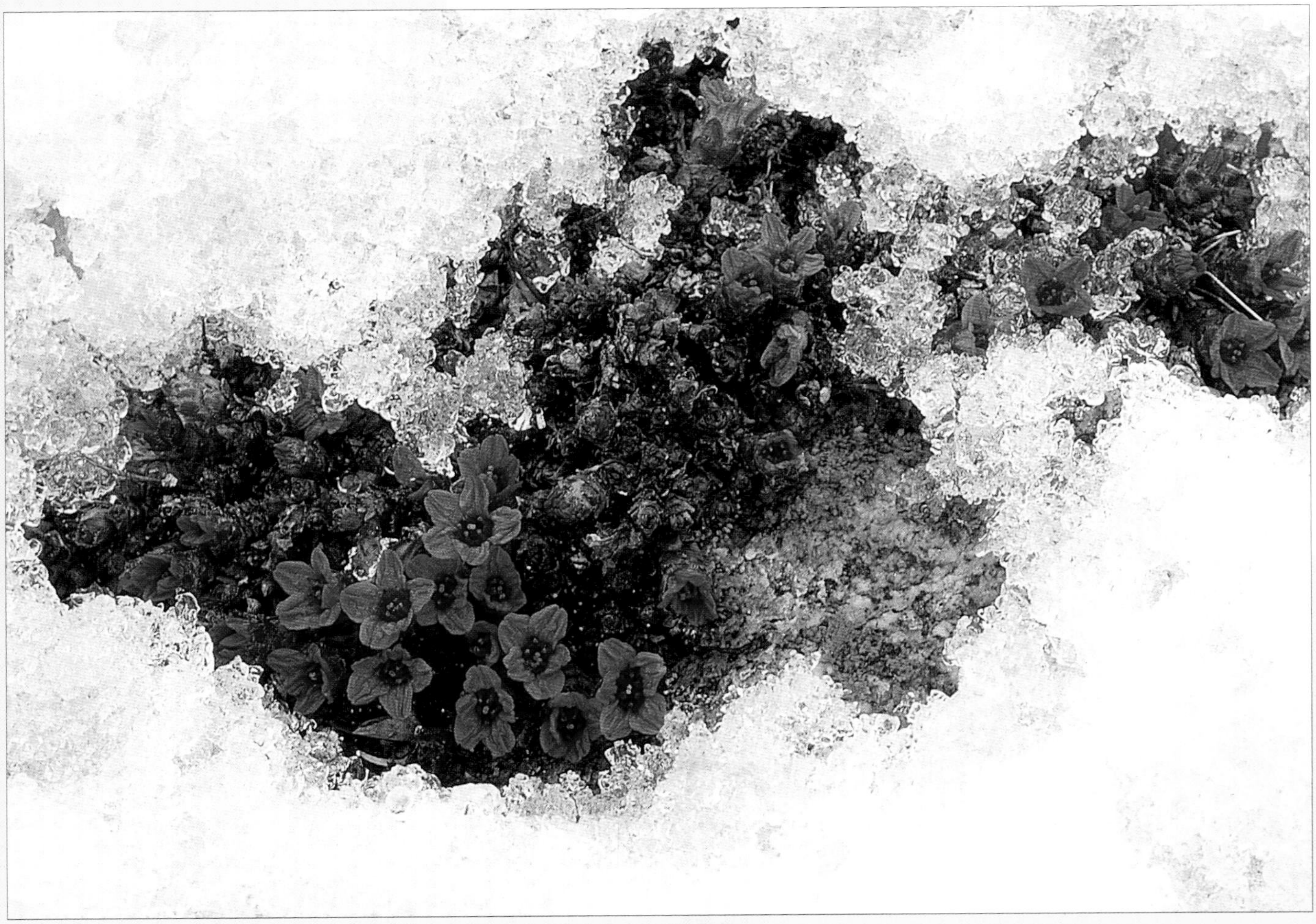

Different life cycles

Plants have evolved a number of different life cycles. Some plants such as marigolds complete their life cycles in one growing season: They grow from seed, flower, produce seeds, and die. Such plants are called annuals. Other plants, such as foxgloves, do the same, except they take two growing seasons to complete their life cycle. They are called biennials. Perennial plants live for more than two seasons. Indeed, some perennials may live for many years before completing their life cycle. Some bristlecone pines in California's White Mountains are more than 4,500 years old. They are probably Earth's oldest plants.

In herbs (or herbaceous perennials), such as peonies, all the foliage above the

▲ *A bristlecone pine tree, one of the oldest known types of tree. They live with little competition from other plants and free from pests and disease.*

CLOSEUP

SPEEDY BREEDERS

The speed at which plants reproduce plays a part in how they compete for space and light. Conifers complete their reproductive cycles over a number of years. That is why in many parts of the world they have been outcompeted by flowering plants, which reproduce much more quickly. Speed is a reproductive strategy (see **8**: 30–41).

CLOSEUP

REACHING FOR THE LIGHT

If you are a plant, one way of reaching the light before your neighbors is to scramble up a nearby tree. That saves you putting all sorts of energy into building a thick, strong trunk.

Some climbing plants such as peas and cucumbers have a stem that is not woody and dies back at the end of the growing season. They are herbaceous. Others, such as grapes and clematis, have woody stems.Woody climbers are sometimes called lianas. Some climbers have thin stemlike structures that are sensitive to touch and wrap around any handy branch or twig they come into contact with. These structures are called tendrils. Others, such as Virginia creeper, have suckers that attach to trees or walls.

Another trick used by some plants is to grow in a crevice high up in a tree where there is plenty of light and where rainwater collects. Such plants are called epiphytes. Many orchids (see below) are epiphytes.

ground dies at the start of winter. When spring comes, new foliage grows up from the ground. In more arid parts of the world herbs die down at the start of the dry season and send up new shoots when the rains return. During the harsh conditions of winter or the dry season herbs keep alive using various kinds of underground structures, such as roots, rhizomes, bulbs, or tubers, to store food.

Competing with others

Plants principally compete with each other for space. Most importantly, plants need light to help them make their own food by photosynthesis (see 6–12). So, many plants try to get as much sunlight on their leaves as possible by outgrowing their neighbors upward. If trees are growing close together, they will not put effort into sending out side branches. Instead, their trunks grow tall

▲ *In a dense tropical rainforest, like this one in Borneo, the trees grow very tall so they can reach the sunlight.*

and thin, and they concentrate their foliage at the top. Competition for sunlight is particularly fierce in tropical forests. There the tops of the trees form a closed cover, or canopy, that may be more than 100 feet (30m) above the ground.

If an old tree dies and falls, there is a desperate race among the seedlings that

APPLICATIONS

FRIENDLY BACTERIA

Plants such as peas, beans, and clover are called legumes. They have developed a close relationship with certain bacteria. These bacteria, called *Rhizobium*, live in the roots of the plants. There the bacteria convert nitrogen from the atmosphere into compounds the legumes are able to use for growth (see **10**: 14). The process is called nitrogen fixing. The plant then changes the nitrogen compounds into proteins, the main building blocks of plant cells.

Legumes do not need artificial fertilizer to get their nitrogen. Farmers can save money on fertilizers by growing legumes on a field in between growing other crops. That gives the soil a rest. And if the legume crop is plowed back into the soil, the earth is enriched with the nitrogen compounds in the legumes.

APPLICATIONS

THE GRASSES: HUMANITY'S BEST FRIEND?

The grass family includes cereal crops that provide a large proportion of the world's population with its staple food. The most important cereals include rice, wheat, millet, corn, oats, barley, and rye.

People first began to plant the seeds of wild barley in western Asia some 10,000 years ago, and this marked the beginning of agriculture. Over the next few thousand years people in Central America began to grow corn, while people in southern China began to grow rice. By selecting the best individual plants from which to collect seeds, people have bred varieties of these crops that produce far more grain than their wild ancestors.

The grasses also play a less direct but still important role in what we eat: Grasses form the main food of grazers such as cattle and sheep, which in turn provide us with meat.

People use barley for making flat bread and porridge, and it can be added to soup. It is also used to feed livestock.

grow in its place to reach the canopy first. Those that are not successful die from lack of sunlight.

Plants also compete for space on the ground, both to get as much light as possible and to get the maximum amount of nutrients and water from the soil. Some plants produce an enormous number of seeds that are blown by the wind, allowing daughter plants to spread over

CLOSEUP

MEAT-EATING PLANTS

In places such as bogs, where the soil is poor in nutrients, some plants have evolved a carnivorous (meat-eating) lifestyle. They catch insects by various crafty tricks. The plants then slowly digest the insects, getting nutrients from their prey. Plants such as sundews and butterworts have the simplest traps. They produce a sticky substance on which the insects get stuck.

More complicated are the traps of pitcher plants. Each is shaped like a vase, and insects are lured inside by a sugary liquid. Once the insect is inside, downward-pointing hairs and a slippery surface stop it from getting out. Perhaps the most extraordinary carnivorous plant is the Venus flytrap. The trap is a pair of hinged, comblike structures with touch-sensitive hairs. When an insect touches the trap, it snaps shut, and the prey is doomed.

A fly caught in a Venus flytrap.

PLANT PARASITES

Some plants do not get their essential nutrients from the soil. Instead, they take them from other plants. Mistletoe is a well known parasitic plant. It grows out of the branches of trees although it does not entirely depend on its host.

The most spectacular plant parasite also has the biggest flower in the world. *Rafflesia*, which grows in the tropical forests of Southeast Asia, has flowers that grow up to 3 feet (1m) across (see above). The plant draws its nutrients from the roots of various vines.

Rafflesia is pollinated by insects (see 36–39), which it attracts by giving off a smell of rotting meat. This has earned the flower the name "stinking-corpse lily." What kind of insects do you think it would attract by giving off a smell like rotting meat?

a wide area. Others plants, such as grasses and strawberries, multiply by sending out side shoots that in turn send down roots into the soil (see 35). That way the plants get to carpet large areas.

Surviving heat and dryness

Although we sometimes think of deserts as dead places because they are so dry, many plants actually thrive there. The big problem is getting water and keeping it. Some

▲ *This mesquite tree can survive dry conditions. It uses its very long single roots to reach underground water up to 50 feet (16m) down.*

desert plants send down very long single roots (called taproots) that reach underground supplies of water. The roots of the mesquite tree, for example, can burrow down more than 50 feet (16m) into the ground. Other plants, such as cacti, spread their matlike roots out over a wide area to take advantage of any rain that falls.

Desert plants such as cacti can store large amounts of water in their fleshy stems. The organ-pipe cactus can hold up to 100 gallons (380 liters) of water. The plant can survive on that amount for

CLOSEUP

POISONING THE NEIGHBORS

Some desert plants, such as creosote bushes, make sure that other plants cannot compete with them for scarce water by poisoning the ground around them. The poison is contained in liquid oozing out of the plant. It kills off any other young plants that try to grow nearby.

PLANT DEFENSES

The most important way in which animals defend themselves from predators is to run away. Plants cannot do that, but have devised a number of different defenses.

The most obvious defense against browsers and grazers is to have spiky leaves or thorn-covered stems or branches. If the animal bites the plant, it gets a nasty shock. Less obvious is the use of chemicals. When they are attacked by hungry insects, some types of trees produce chemicals that repel the attackers. Some trees even send a chemical signal through the air to other trees of the same species. The other trees are able to get their chemical defenses ready even before the insect horde arrives.

► ***The ribs of an organ pipe cactus cast cooling shadows onto the plant's surface.***

four months without rain. Cacti also save water by reducing their leaves to tiny spines (see 11). That gives the plant a much smaller surface area from which water can evaporate (turn into water vapor). The spines also cast many small shadows over the surface of the cactus, helping it keep cool. The ribs on many cacti perform the same function (see right), as does the pale green or gray color of many desert plants.

Surviving the cold

The farther north you go in North America (and also in Europe and Asia), the more the forests are dominated by conifers such as spruce, pine, and fir. The same happens as

ANT ASSOCIATES

Many plants share close relationships with ants. Ant-house plants (below), for example, have swollen roots filled with chambers. Some house an ant colony. Other chambers are used by the ants as trash dumps. The plants aborb nutrients from the trash. Plants have many deadly insect enemies, such as caterpillars that munch their leaves. Some plants fight off such pests with the help of ant bodyguards. The ants attack the pests and often get a safe place to live in return. Acacia ants are extremely fierce. They live inside hollow thorns on acacia trees. The trees even feed their ant lodgers. They provide small, nutritious buttons of food, as well as sugary nectar.

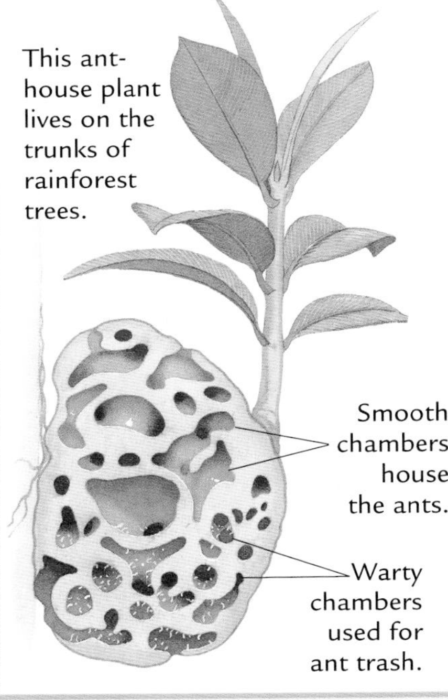

This ant-house plant lives on the trunks of rainforest trees.

you climb higher in the world's mountain ranges. That is because conifers have many features that help them survive long, cold winters better than broad-leaved trees such as maple, oak, and hickory.

Most conifers have evergreen leaves, so they can take advantage of sunlight as soon as conditions become favorable for photosynthesis (see 6–12). The leaves themselves are needlelike, which helps prevent the trees from being damaged when it is windy or during severe frosts. The roots of conifers do not go deep into the ground. That is important in cold northern climates since the soil only a few feet down is permanently frozen.

Farther north than the great coniferous forests, and above the tree line in the high

HOT DEBATE

WILD FIRE

People often think of forest fires as bad things. We blame careless picnickers or a discarded cigarette and spend thousands of hours and millions of dollars each year trying to put out fires.

However, fires caused by lightning have always been a natural and regular feature of some types of forests. Most conifer trees retain leaves throughout the year, and they bear cones containing new seeds. Conifers are also full of resins that burn very easily. But heat also triggers their cones to open and shed their seeds. The seeds, in turn, grow into new conifer trees.

In some areas, such as the dense, thorny scrubland or chaparral of California, fires are also a regular natural feature. Many of the scrubby plants, such as chamiso and manzanita, are full of volatile oils that burn easily. Fire can burn these plants, and it also clears low ground cover. That is helpful because fire is necessary to make the seeds of many chaparral plants germinate (sprout). The seedlings then take advantage of the cleared ground.

mountains, plants have had to adapt to even more extreme conditions. Most, even those that grow tall elsewhere, are low growing. That way they are protected from ice particles whipped along by the fierce winds. Many plants, such as saxifrages, grow into cushion shapes. That keeps them warmer inside.

▲ *On mountains dwarf willows grow low to avoid strong winds.*

COPING WITH THE SEASONS

In parts of the world with warm summers and cold winters many trees drop their leaves in the fall. The tree then enters a period of inactivity called dormancy in the same way that some animals hibernate in winter.

In woodland many small ground plants, such as wild columbine and blue and yellow violets, shoot up and flower in early spring, before the leaves of the trees grow back and cut off much of the sunlight. In contrast, the climate in tropical forests is more constant all year round, so many of the trees are evergreen. The leaves on any one tree fall at different times.

The red trillium flowers in woodland in spring.

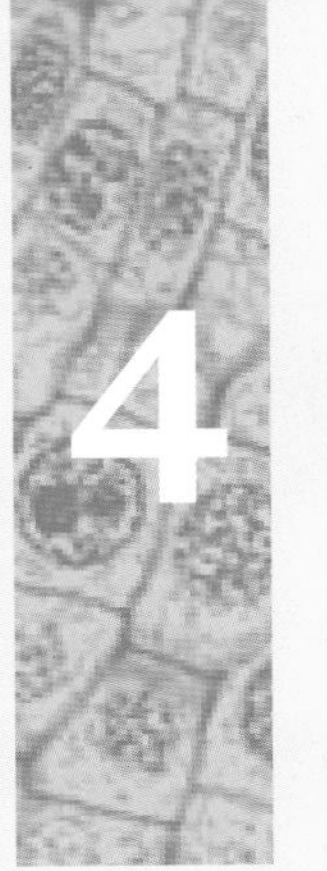

4 Hormones and Coordination

Plant hormones are chemicals in plants that help them develop and respond to the outside world.

Plant roots grow downward. Stem shoots grow upward. Flowers form and fruit ripens at the appropriate time of year. Seedlings grow toward a bright light. An upturned root turns downward to the pull of gravity. How are plants able to do these things without a brain, a nervous system, or sense organs? The answer is by making chemicals called plant hormones inside the plant.

◀ *The roots of a plant grow downward, while the shoots grow upward. That happens because of plant hormones.*

Meristems

Plants grow by making new cells in areas called meristems. The most important meristems are near the tips of roots and shoots, and near the edges of leaves. Other meristems cause stems to grow thicker or produce the cells that form fruits and flowers. Some meristems continue to

WHAT DO PLANT HORMONES DO?

HORMONE	MAIN EFFECT	EXAMPLES
Abscisic acid	• Response to stress. • Seed dormancy.	• Responses to water stress (drought), wounding, and disease. • Stops seeds from germinating before they have separated from the parent plant.
Auxin	Growth.	• Increase in length of shoots and roots. • Response to light and gravity.
Cytokinin	Cell division (see **2**: 52–61).	Growth of leaves, roots, and stems.
Ethylene	• Fruit ripening. • Leaf fall.	Ripening in fruits like bananas, apples, and tomatoes.
Gibberellin	Control of growth.	• Final height of the plant. • Developing flowers.

make new cells for the whole life of the plant. Others are temporary. Plant hormones control meristem activity and so control plant growth.

How many plant hormones are there?

Up until the 1970s scientists knew about five plant hormones: auxin, gibberellin, ethylene, cytokinin, and abscisic acid. More recently, scientists found that some other hormones control plant growth too. Some plant hormones do specific jobs, but others are essential for many aspects of plant growth.

The table above shows the main effects of five plant hormones. Two of them, auxin and cytokinin, are essential for the life of all plant tissues. The effects of auxin, gibberellin, and ethylene are described in more detail later (see 26–30).

THE ROLE OF AUXIN

Experiments show that the plant hormone auxin causes the cells that grow in a wound to change into water-transporting xylem tissue (see 9). Scientists wounded a cucumber stem, then added auxin to a bud near the wound. When the experimenters cut the stem into thin sections and studied it under a light microscope, they saw that lines of xylem cells had grown across the wound.

AUXIN AND LEAVES

If a leaf blade is cut off a plant and no auxin is added (**1**), the petiole (a stem that supports the leaf blade) falls off. However, if a blade is removed, and auxin is added, the petiole stays on the plant (**2**).

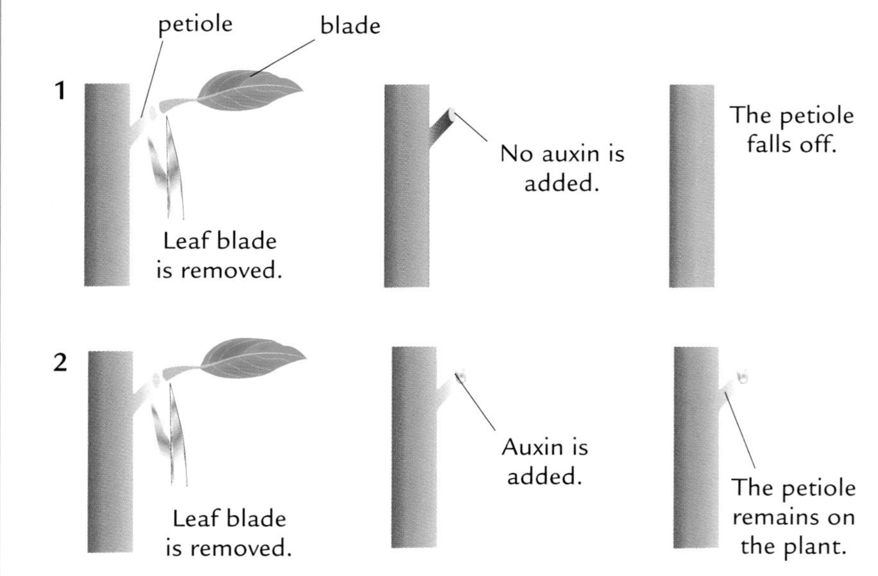

THE EFFECT OF AUXIN

Auxin is produced in the seeds on the outside of a strawberry. That makes the fruit grow. In the middle picture the seeds have been removed from the outside, leaving a tiny fruit. In the right-hand picture auxin has been added to a strawberry without seeds, and it has grown almost as big as the fruit with all its seeds (left-hand picture).

Hormones and cells

Plant cells each have a specific job to do. For instance, the cells that are on the outside protect the rest of the plant. Inside the plant other cells form pipes or tubes that transport water and nutrients (see 9-13). Some plant cells change what they do during the lifetime of the plant. Hormones control which jobs plant cells do and when they change jobs.

A good example is the process of leaf fall (abscission). When a leaf drops from the plant, special cells in the leaf stalk change so they are no longer attached to the cells next to them. One plant hormone, auxin, slows down the changes so the leaf stays attached to the plant for longer. Another hormone, ethylene, causes the cells to change so they separate from the cells next to them. That makes the leaf fall earlier (see 29).

Controlling what cells do is an important function for hormones. Without them plants would be unable to function or to show such a range of shapes and colors.

Hormones and plant shape

The meristem at the top of a plant's main stem grows more quickly than any of the side branches. That is called apical dominance. It produces the characteristic cone shape of many plants (see right).

The main stem is dominant because it produces the plant hormone auxin, which inhibits (slows) the growth of other stems. If the main stem is damaged and loses its tip, thus destroying the meristem, the side branches grow more quickly. Other hormones also play a role. Cytokinin promotes cell division (see **2**: 52-61) If you apply cytokinin to a side branch, it will grow rapidly even if the main stem is producing auxin.

Hormones and bending

In the 1870s British naturalist Charles Darwin (1809–1882) and his son Francis (1848–1925) studied how shoots grow toward light. They found that when very young canary grass seedlings were illuminated from one side, they grew toward the light.

▲ *Fir trees have a typical cone shape. It is due to apical dominance, meaning that the area at the top of the plant grows faster than the side branches.*

DARWIN'S EXPERIMENT

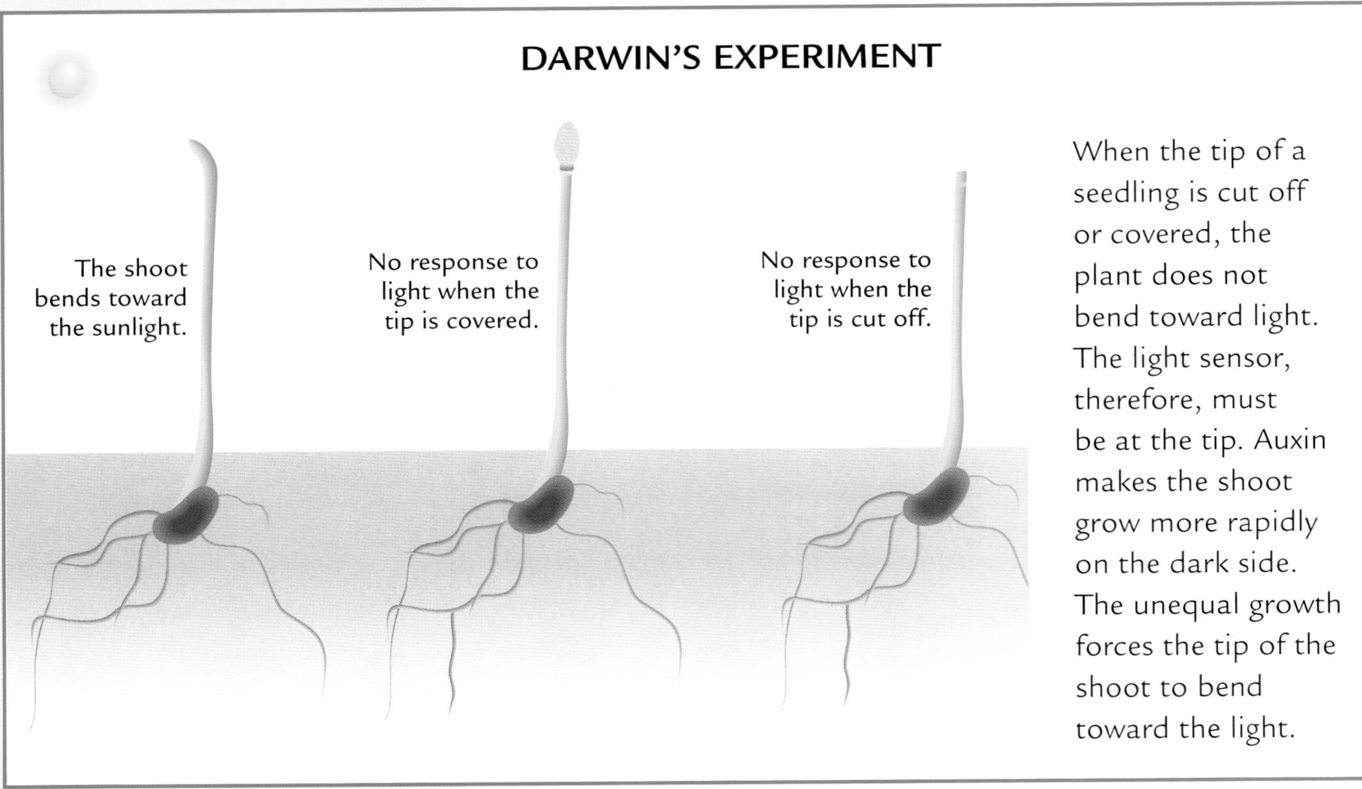

When the tip of a seedling is cut off or covered, the plant does not bend toward light. The light sensor, therefore, must be at the tip. Auxin makes the shoot grow more rapidly on the dark side. The unequal growth forces the tip of the shoot to bend toward the light.

This is called a tropism, which is a growth response toward or away from a stimulus such as light or gravity. When Darwin cut off or covered the top of the seedling, it no longer grew toward the light (see above).

Plants have a photoreceptor (area sensitive to light) at the tip of the shoot. It detects

◀ *Tomatoes at different stages of ripening. The ones at the bottom are still unripe and green; the middle ones are yellow, and the top ones are red and fully ripe. Ethylene gas is the plant hormone that stimulates the ripening process.*

the direction of a light source, usually the sun. The plant hormone auxin makes the seedling grow more quickly on the dark side, which causes the seedling to bend toward the light. That is phototropism.

Auxin also controls tropism in roots. The roots bend toward gravity, which is usually downward. The gravity receptor is a series of heavy molecules that occur inside gravity-sensing cells called statocytes.

Today tropisms are investigated using plants that are genetically modified (see **3**: 64) so that the response does not work properly. These studies produce information about the parts of the plant that can detect light and gravity. The studies also demonstrate the way auxin controls growth. Experiments carried out on the Space Shuttle have investigated how plants respond to the zero gravity of space flight.

Hormones and ripe fruit

The plant hormone ethylene is a gas. In the early 1900s people discovered that bananas ripened well if carried in vans heated by coke stoves, while those carried in electrically heated vehicles did not. The ripening trigger was ethylene, a gas produced by coke stoves but not electric heaters.

TRY THIS

FALLING LEAVES

Ripening fruits produce ethylene gas. The gas causes nearby fruit to ripen. It also triggers the fall of leaves. You can test that using holly.

You will need two jars you can seal tightly, a ripe apple, two sprigs of holly, and two small pots of water. Put the jars on a warm windowsill. Put a small pot of water into each of the jars, and stand the holly stems in the water (**1**). Put the apple into one of the jars before sealing them both. After a week the leaves from the holly sprig in the jar containing the apple will drop off (**2**). That is because the ethylene gas from the apple makes the holly shed its leaves.

In the top picture (**1**) the holly leaves are attached to the stalk. In the lower picture (**2**) the jar contains a ripe apple, and the holly leaves have fallen off.

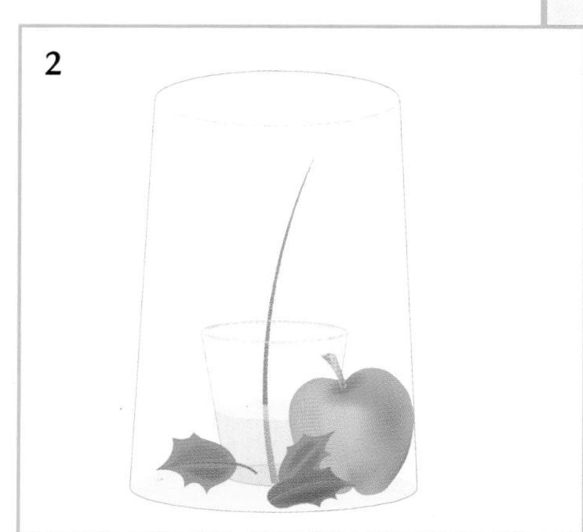

SEEDLESS GRAPES

Normally the seeds in grapes produce the hormone gibberellic acid, which makes the fruit develop. If the growers spray the grape plants with gibberellic acid, the fruit can develop without seeds. The growers also surround the plants with steam to kill the cells that take sugars and hormones down to the roots. The fruit uses the hormones and sugars to grow bigger and juicier.

◀ *The small cabbages on the left of the picture were grown on cool, short days with long nights. When the plants on the right were given the hormone gibberellin, they grew rapidly upward and began to flower.*

Ethylene speeds up ripening in some fruit, including bananas, apples, pears, and tomatoes. Fruiting plants produce their own ethylene naturally. It enables the fruit to ripen at the same time because ethylene produced by a ripe fruit will speed up ripening in other, less ripe fruit. Fruit growers control ethylene levels carefully when bananas are being transported to make sure the fruits ripen just in time to go on sale.

Long days and tall plants

Many plants sense and respond to day length. A good example is the cabbage. When the day is short and the night long, a cabbage develops leaves near the ground; this is the cabbage we buy in a supermarket. If days are long and nights are short, the same cabbage grows tall and produces flowering stalks. Gardeners call this bolting. Gibberellin is the plant hormone that controls bolting. Plants make more gibberellin on long days and are then more likely to bolt.

Genetic engineering

Plant biotechnology companies want to produce large numbers of genetically identical plants (clones). Some of them are genetically engineered to do new things. Others may be copies of a particularly useful plant. In the process called micropropagation small pieces of a plant are grown in sterile containers

CLONING PLANTS

A piece of plant material is cultured with nutrients and the plant hormones cytokinin and auxin. It is then exposed to different combinations and concentrations of auxin and cytokinin. Roots and shoots form. Finally, plantlets are ready to be planted in soil.

Plants are grown in sterile plastic containers on shelves under fluorescent lights inside a room for cloning thousands of identical plants. The temperature is kept at 70 °F (22 °C), which is ideal for growth. Clones of plants are grown in plastic tissue culture jars. In this way many small plants can be reared in sterile conditions in a small space.

with nutrients and hormones (see box above). Plants that are micropropagated include potatoes, orchids, bananas, and even forest trees.

If the plant is genetically engineered with a foreign gene added, all the clones contain the new gene. Micropropagation is essential for the commercial production of genetically modified crops.

Crops engineered with foreign genes can tolerate herbicides (weed killers), so that farmers can use new methods of weed control. Plants can be made to resist damage by insects like the Colorado potato beetle. Scientists also add genes that permit plants to grow in hostile environments, or that result in the production of useful antibiotics.

▶ *Workers prepare graft clones of cacao leaves in Ecuador. The tips are dipped into an enzyme and then planted for rooting. Through cloning, all of the cacao on this plantation is of the same variety. Cacao makes chocolate.*

HOT DEBATE

WHAT ARE HORMONES?

Is "hormone" the right name for the chemicals that control plant growth? In the 1980s plant biologist Tony Trewavas (1939–) suggested the alternative name "plant growth substance." Why? Animal hormones have only a few functions each, but plant hormones do many different things. Take auxin for example. It works with other hormones, controlling growth and responses to gravity and light, and determining the function of particular cells.

Many scientists still use the word "hormone." But are they right, or does it just confuse people into thinking that plant hormones act like animal hormones?

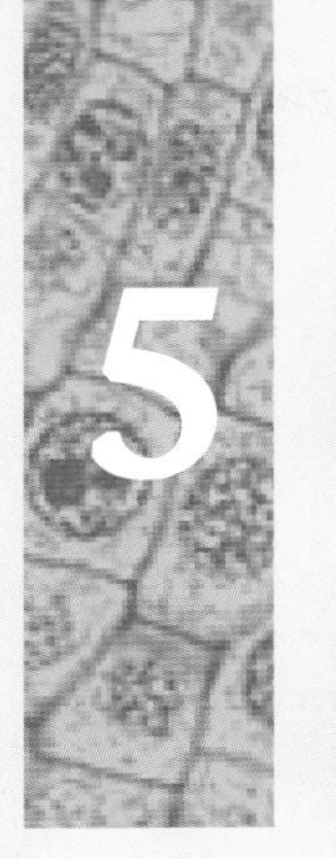

5 Reproduction and Propagation

Plants use ways of reproducing or propagating (increasing their numbers) to ensure their genes pass on.

Reproduction ensures that a plant's genes (inherited information, see 3: 34) move into future generations. In plants reproduction involves the formation of either seeds or microscopic spores. Spore-producing plants include ferns and mosses. The fossil record (see 9: 8–10) shows that reproduction by spores first developed in the Silurian period, around 420 million years ago (see 9: 55). Flowering plants, conifers, and their relatives reproduce by making seeds. Plants probably evolved seeds much later, in the Carboniferous period, around 300 million years ago.

▼ *Moss spore capsules contain spores. After the capsules open, the spores grow into new plants.*

Asexual reproduction

Some plants produce spores asexually, by budding tissues. Thousands of spores develop in this way inside a spore case. When the spore case breaks open, the spores are released. Since they are so tiny, even the gentlest air currents can carry them some distance from the parent plant. If the

WHAT IS A SPECIES?

Taxonomy is the study of plants' and animals' relationships with one another. Species are the basic unit of taxonomy. The most common definition of a species is a group of organisms that is unable to reproduce with another group to produce fertile offspring (see **1**: 16–23). So leopards, robins, and people are all species.

While this definition works well for most animals, it does not do so well with plants. Plants of two different species can sometimes produce offspring. They are called hybrids, and they are usually fertile. If the definition of a species were accurate, they would not be able to do so.

There are many examples of plants that crossbreed across species boundaries. For example, some types of cotton that are now grown commercially are the result of accidental crosses between different species of cotton.

Some crossbreeds are the product of quite distantly related species. The Russian botanist (plant scientist) G. D. Karpechenko (1899–1941) crossbred a cabbage and a radish. The plant was not grown commercially because it had the leaves of a radish and the roots of a cabbage.

Scientists are starting to agree that new definitions of species may be needed for different kinds of plants.

spores land on suitable habitat, they germinate (sprout). Their next step is to grow into the gametophyte stage. Gametes (sex cells) form, fuse, and go into the sporophyte stage, which then produces spores.

Sexual reproduction

Sexual reproduction in plants is similar to animal reproduction in one way: It involves

▶ *Ferns like this Maidenhair have leaves called fronds. The brown dots are cases that contain the plant's spores.*

the fusion of male and female sex cells. A cell with the plant's normal number of chromosomes (gene-containing structures) is formed from the fusion of two cells, usually a pollen grain that contains a male sex cell and a female ovule, each with half the normal number of chromosomes.

GM CROPS AND POLLINATION

Genetically modified (GM) crops are big news. Scientists, farmers, politicians, and environmentalists are arguing about whether GM plants are good or bad (see **4**: 62). Some people support the production of GM crops because they can reduce the damage to plants caused by diseases and pests. That means higher yields are possible. However, some people think the negative aspects of GM crops outweigh the positive ones.

Many environmentalists believe that pollen from GM crops may crossfertilize wild relatives of that crop. The resulting offspring may be "superweeds" that are no use as crops and cannot be killed by chemicals called herbicides. The offspring may also provide no food for insects and other wildlife, whose numbers may decline as a result. Some studies have shown that these concerns are justified, but a lot more research is needed.

STRUCTURE OF A FLOWER

Some plants have separate male and female flowers, but others such as this one (right) combine the two. The male parts are called the stamens. The anther holds the pollen, ready for release into the wind or onto an insect's body. The female parts are called the carpel. Pollen from another flower lands on the stigma. Each pollen grain then grows a tube inside the style. Male sex cells move through the tubes and reach the ovary. There the male sex cells fertilize the ovules, leading to the development of seeds. The sepals provide support for the flower, while the petals may bear markings that guide in insects.

petal
stamen
anther
filament
sepal
stigma
style
carpel
ovary
ovules

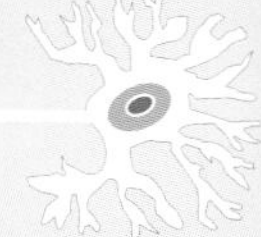

Most animals can move, search for mates, and seek a suitable habitat for their offspring to grow up in. Plants cannot move, so they rely on wind, water, or animals to carry their male sex cells (inside pollen in seed-bearing plants) to the female receptive surface, called the stigma.

Most animals are either male or female, but most plants can function both as male and female; they are hermaphrodites. There are exceptions, though. Some species of plants have male individuals and female individuals. They are dioecious plants: Spinach, hollies, and ginkgos are examples.

Pollen dispersal

In seed plants the spreading of pollen from the male parts to the female parts is called pollination. In most nonflowering seed plants such as conifers and in some flowering plants pollination occurs

TRY THIS

VEGETATIVE REPRODUCTION

Many plants practice sexual reproduction. That means the pollen of one plant fertilizes the ovule of another. Most plants can also reproduce asexually without this crossfertilization taking place. Asexual reproduction in plants is called vegetative reproduction. It produces free-growing plants that are genetically identical to the parent plants. The offspring is a clone of its parent.

How does asexual reproduction occur? Many houseplants, such as geraniums, can be vegetatively reproduced from pieces of stem. Money plants will easily grow from bits of leaf.

Fill a small plant pot with damp potting soil, and press a geranium stem 1 inch (2.5cm) into the soil. Lightly press a money plant leaf into the surface of the soil in another pot. Put the pots near a windowsill, out of direct sunlight. Roots will start growing from the stem and the leaf within a week or two, followed by new leaves. Gardeners frequently use these reproductive methods to grow new plants.

Strawberry plants can reproduce vegetatively. The main plants produce runners, or stolons, which develop roots. The parent plant provides food through the runners, and complete new plants form.

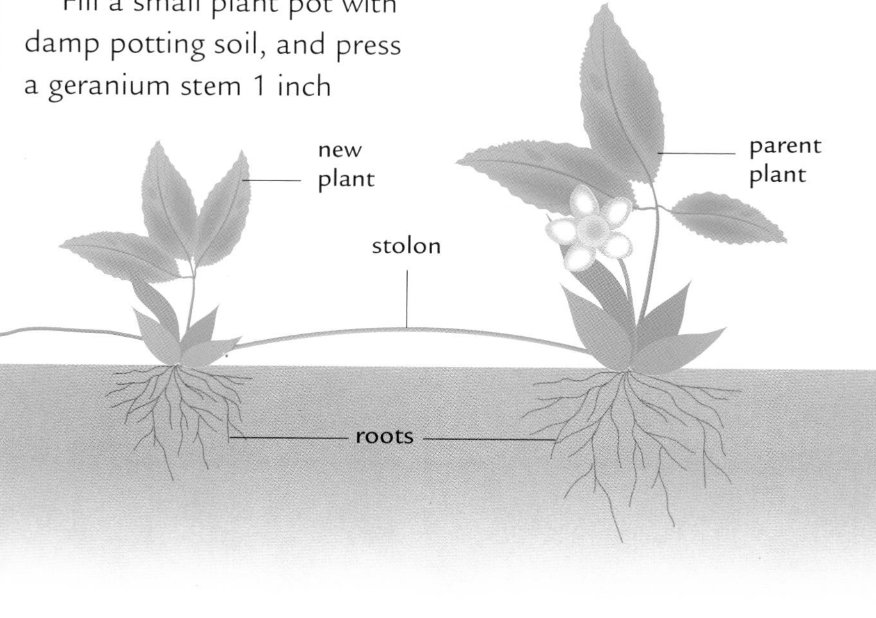

INTO THE PAST

THE DISCOVERY OF POLLINATION

The principles of pollination were known to ancient Greek and Roman writers even in the 4th century B.C. Theophrastus (c. 371–c. 286 B.C.) observed that the fruit of the date palm was only produced by female plants, and that fruit production was better if "dust" (pollen) from the male plant was shaken onto the female flowers. After the invention of the microscope in the 17th century (see **1**: 50) botanists could study tiny pollen grains. Around this time a number of different European botanists started investigating the link between insects that visited flowers and plant reproduction.

when pollen is carried by the wind. This is called wind pollination.

A small number of aquatic flowering plants use water currents in the same way; that is called water pollination (see 37). In more than 95 percent of flowering plants animal carriers take male pollen to the stigma of another plant. Many different types of animals can act as carriers, including bees, flies, beetles, butterflies, moths, bats, birds, and lizards.

All animal-pollinated flowers work in much the same way: They attract animals with their bright color or strong scent. Animals associate these features with a reward, usually nectar (a sweet liquid) or protein-rich pollen. When collecting the reward, the animal brushes against the flower's anthers (see 34).

Anthers are part of the plant's male sex organs. They contain pollen and are at the end of thin filaments. As the animal brushes the anthers, pollen gets attached to the animal's body. If it moves to another flower, the animal may brush against a stigma. The pollen can then be transferred. The animal that carries the pollen is called a pollinator. The relationship between the plant and its

◀ *Pollen grains (magnified). A pollen grain has a diameter between 10 micrometers (μm) and 200 μm (there are 1,000 μm in 1 millimeter). Pollen forms in the anthers of seed-producing plants. Each grain produces two male sex cells.*

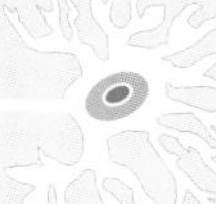

Hornwort is an underwater flowering plant. Pollen is carried in the water from plant to plant.

Animals such as this bat can carry pollen from the male flowers to the female flowers.

pollinator is called a mutualism since both the plant and the pollinator benefit (see **6**: 58–59).

Fertilization

However it arrives, whether by wind, water, or animal transport, the pollen becomes glued to the stigma. Each grain of pollen then sends out a long pollen tube. The pollen tube grows down inside the style, which connects the stigma to the ovules in the ovary (see 34). The ovules can then be fertilized.

POLLINATION SYNDROMES

Have you ever wondered why the flowers of plants have different odors, shapes, and colors? Different types of flowers attract different insects and animals. For instance, many flowers that are pollinated by moths are white, scented, have long tubes, and open at night, when most moths are active. Bird-pollinated flowers are often red and have no scent because birds have good red vision but a poor sense of smell. These flowers produce a sugar-rich, energy-giving liquid called nectar. Birds need a lot of energy to fly, so they are attracted to red flowers to feed on the nectar.

The idea that different types of flowers attract different carriers of their pollen was first explained by the Italian botanist Frederico Delpino (1833–1905) in the 19th century. He called the different combinations of color, scent, and shape pollination syndromes. Delpino's ideas are still used by many biologists who study pollination, but some disagree about how useful his system is for classifying flowers.

HOW COMMON ARE POLLINATION SYNDROMES?

Flowers of some plants can be easily grouped into pollination syndromes. The syndromes are based on combinations of flower color, shape, and scent. This classification system has been used for about 150 years in studying flower evolution.

Recently scientists have started to question just how common these pollination syndromes are in nature. There are many plants that do not comfortably fit into one category or another. It may be that people have tried to classify nature too neatly, forgetting about flowers that do not fit into the syndromes.

Scientists have studied the pollination of fewer than 1 percent of the quarter of a million or more flowering plants alive today. There is still much for us to learn about plants and their pollinators.

DARWIN'S ORCHID

British naturalist Charles Darwin (1809–1882) studied the evolution of flowers and their pollinators (see 28). He used examples of plant reproduction in his book *On the Origin of Species* (1859). In 1862 Darwin predicted that an orchid growing in Madagascar, which had a flower tube 11 inches (28 cm) long, would be pollinated by a moth with a tongue the same length. Forty years later Darwin was proved right. The scientists who discovered the moth named it *Xanthopan morgani praedicta* in honor of Darwin's prediction: *Praedicta* is Latin for "predicted."

The pollen tube is attracted to chemical signals produced by the ovules. Once it reaches the ovule, the pollen tube enters through an opening in the ovule called the micropyle. Inside the ovule one of the male sex cells fuses with the nucleus of the female sex cell. This is plant fertilization. It is the same principle as what

▼ *A broad-billed hummingbird pollinates as it uses its long beak to gather nectar from a flower.*

SEED DISPERSAL STRATEGIES

Plants use many different methods to ensure their seeds are carried away from the parent plant. During summer and fall look around your backyard, local park, or out in the countryside. Observe any fruit and seeds that you see, and make a list of all the different ways that seeds are moved.

Seeds often lie within brightly colored fruit with sweet flesh, such as blackberries and hawthorn berries. Birds and mammals are attracted to these fruits since they provide an important source of food. The animals swallow the fruit, digest the flesh, and drop the indigestible seeds out in their feces. The animals may carry the seeds a long way from the parent plant.

Other plants have seeds that are sticky or have tiny hooks: They are carried by mammals in another way. The seeds become attached to mammals' fur and may not fall off until the animal has traveled some way. Cleaver and beggar tick seeds are spread in this way.

The seeds of dandelions have parachutes. So when they are caught by the wind, they float away from the parent plant. Maple seeds are also carried by the wind; they have wings that carry them away from the maple tree. Some plants, such as vetches, have explosive seed pods that catapult their seeds several feet away.

Once a seed finds itself in a suitable habitat, it begins to take up water to germinate.

▲ *Burdock seeds have hooks that attach to people or animals. Then the seeds are carried from one place to another.*

occurs between a male animal's sperm and the egg of a female animal (see 8: 16–29).

Growth of the embryo

The fused pollen and ovule create a single fertilized cell called a zygote. This cell repeatedly splits to form a developing embryo inside a seed. During this time the parent plant nourishes the seed. The parent provides all its water, mineral nutrients, and energy. While the seed

▶ *Dandelion seeds get blown around by the wind. This strategy is called wind dispersal.*

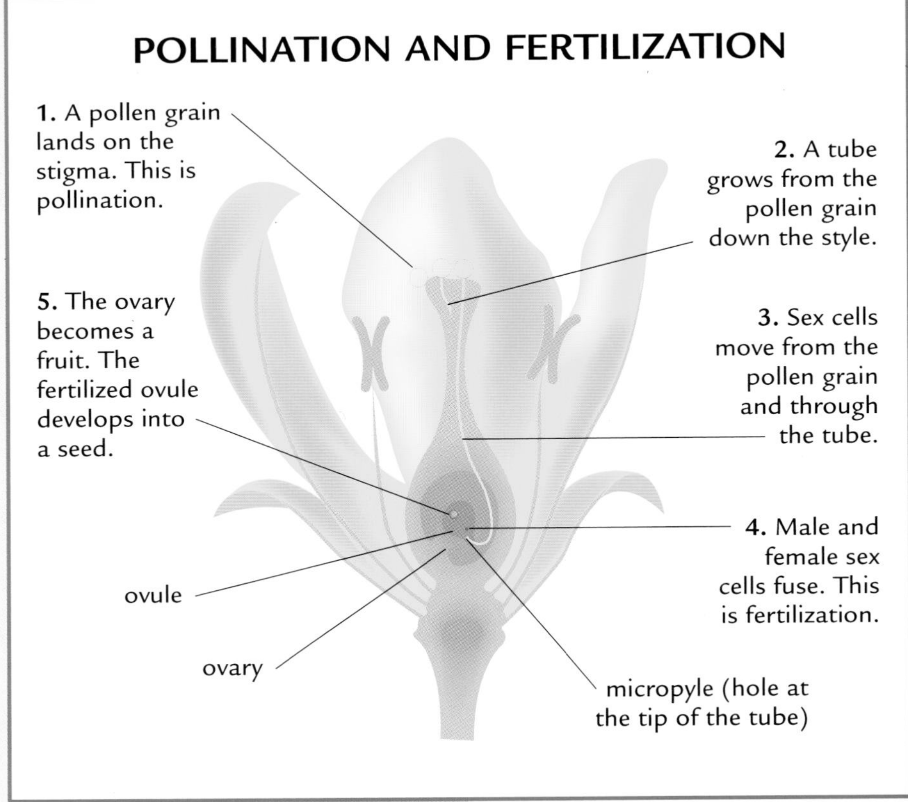

matures, it gradually becomes less dependent on its parent, until it is a self-contained individual, ready to grow in the outside world. When a seed starts to grow shoots and roots (see 41), it has germinated, or sprouted. Some seeds require exposure to a long cold period before germination. That process is called vernalization. Vernalization ensures that the seeds sprout after the harsh weather of winter has passed. Other seeds are sensitive to light and need to be exposed to the sun or to the darkness of the soil before germination.

CYCLES

Once a seed has sprouted, the seedling rapidly grows up toward the light. If the seedling survives disease, grazing animals, and harsh weather, it will eventually reach a size at which it can reproduce and start the whole cycle again. For some plants maturity may come only a few months after they germinate. After they reproduce, they die. They are called annual plants. Other plants grow for two growing seasons, then they reproduce and die. These kinds of plants are called biennials.

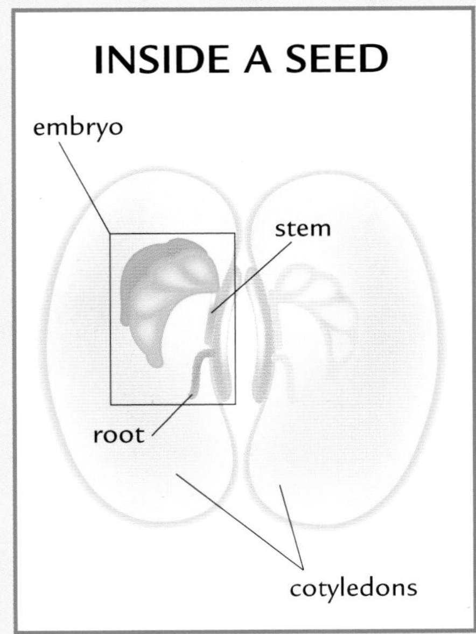

◄ *After fertilization a plant embryo forms inside the seed. The cotyledons provide food for the growing embryo. Later the seed germinates and can start growing in soil.*

Some plants bear fruit only once and may take up to 30 years to reach sexual maturity. They are called monocarpic plants, and they die after shedding their seeds. An example is Pitcher's thistle, a threatened species growing on the sand dunes of the Great Lakes.

Most plants take anything from 1 to 100 years before they are sexually mature. After that they reproduce more or less every year. They are called perennial plants.

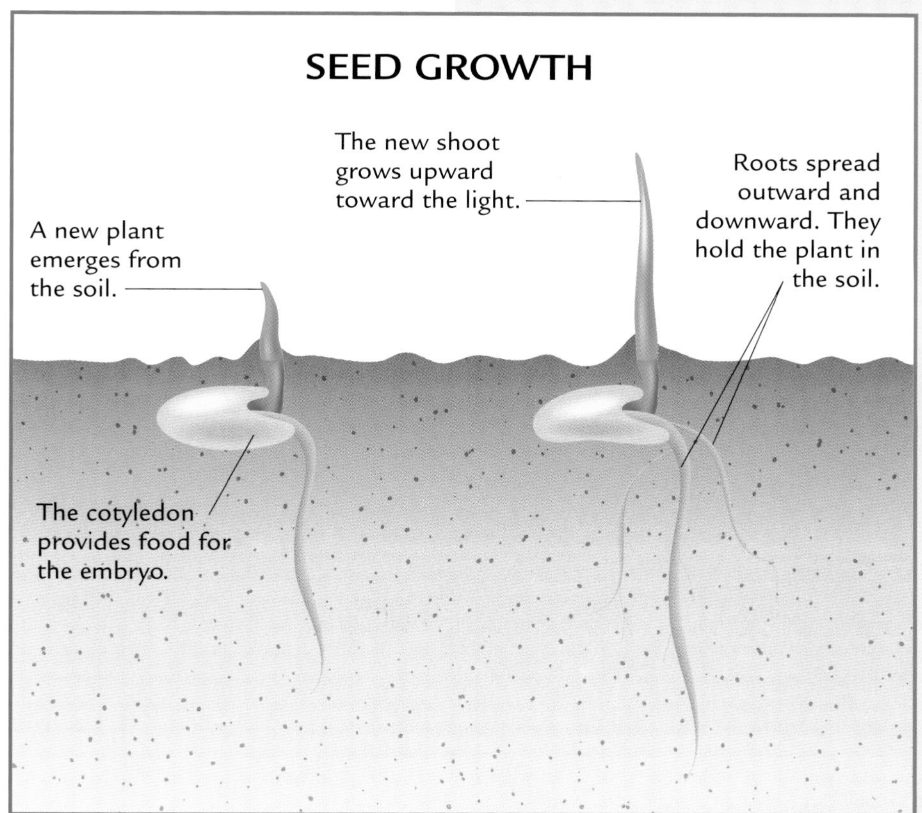

Alternation of generations

There are some differences between reproduction by seeds and by spores, but there is one

TRY THIS

SCARIFYING SEEDS

If all the seeds produced by a plant were to germinate at the same time, they might be attacked by disease or eaten by a grazing animal. The rate of seed germination is slowed down by some plants. Their seeds require the slitting or rubbing away of the seed case before they will germinate. This is called scarification. During scarification the seed coat is damaged in some way, often by mineral particles rubbing against it while it is in the soil. You can experiment with this using dried peas and beans.

Choose five or six different types, such as kidney beans or peas. Select 20 seeds of each type, and divide them into two groups of 10. One set of 10 will be your experimental group; the other set will be your control group (see **1**: 57). Take each seed from your experimental sets, and rub it firmly on sandpaper until a patch of seed coat is worn away. Place each of your sets of 10 seeds onto wet paper towel in the bottom of a shallow bowl, and label them according to whether they were part of your experimental group or part of the control group.

Put the bowls onto a windowsill, and cover them with clear plastic wrap. Over the next week record how many seeds in each group have germinated on each day. Were the scarified seeds faster at germinating than the control seeds?

NEW PLANTS FROM OLD

To create new varieties of crop plants by crossbreeding, scientists who work in agriculture need a good understanding of how plants reproduce. By breeding new plants, the scientists are changing the genetic makeup (genotype) of the plants, so that the features (called the phenotype) turn out to be what they are looking for (see **3**: 61). The features could be earlier, later, or longer flowering time, resistance to disease, tolerance of wet, dry, cold, or hot weather, larger fruit or seeds, shorter or longer stems, and a lot of other desirable characteristics.

important similarity: Both methods of reproduction involve something called the alternation of generations. That is the occurrence of two different stages in the life cycle of these plants. In one stage (the haploid stage) the cells have one set of chromosomes. A chromosome is the part of an organism's cell that

◀ *Kariba hybrids are a new type of tulip. They differ from traditional varieties in color and shape. Kariba tulips were produced through crossfertilization between a number of existing strains.*

carries the genes. Genes give the animal or plant its characteristics (see **3**: 27–29). The chromosomes determine color, shape, and other things. The other stage (the diploid stage) is when the cells have the two sets of chromosomes. In flowering plants the haploid stage of the life cycle is represented by the plants' male sex cells, which are inside the pollen, and their female sex cells, inside the ovules.

◀ *Wild teasel is an example of a biennial plant. It grows for two growing seasons then reproduces and dies.*

WHAT DO YOU THINK?

WHY DO PLANTS FLOWER AT DIFFERENT TIMES OF THE YEAR?

We expect to see certain plants in flower at particular times of the year: snowdrops in winter (below), violets and daffodils in the early spring, cannas later in the summer, and asters in fall.

Why do different species of plants flower at different times of the year? Are they trying to attract pollinators that only appear during certain seasons?

Woodland plants such as wild columbine often flower before the trees produce their leaves. Why do you think that is? Do they need sunlight to produce energy to flower?

6 Plants and People

People and plants have shared a long and very close relationship. People use plants and extracts from their leaves, seeds, and roots in an amazing variety of ways.

There are food plants like potatoes, rice, and corn, while others, such as foxgloves, provide medicines and other drugs. One of the most important plant products, wood, has been used for thousands of years in construction and as a fuel. Plants like cotton and hemp are harvested for fibers from leaves or seed heads. Such fibers make cloth, thread, or ropes. The hundreds of other plant products include varnishes, dyes, and rubber.

FOOD PLANTS

Plants provide us with all of our food, either directly

◀ *A man harvests turnips that he has grown in his yard. Both the roots and the tops of turnips are edible.*

from crops, or indirectly through plant-eating animals. Over thousands of years hundreds of edible plant species have been domesticated (cultivated for human use). However, just 12 species provide more than three-quarters of all the food eaten worldwide today. These vital species are all either grasses, like wheat, or tubers, like potatoes.

Why has our diet become so restricted? It may be because these staple crops were among the earliest to be domesticated. People selected and bred the best varieties over a long time (see **3**: 61). These plants were more productive and easier to farm than plants cultivated from the wild.

Staple crops share several features. They must produce lots of food that matures quickly, is not poisonous, and

THE ORIGINS OF AGRICULTURE

For thousands of years people around the world fed themselves by hunting wild animals or foraging for fruits, tubers, and seeds. However, around 10,000 years ago people began to collect, plant, and grow the seeds of wild plants such as wheat and rice in several different regions. Examples include Mesopotamia (modern-day Iraq), the Indus Valley (modern-day Pakistan), China (below), and Egypt. Rather than wandering far and wide in search of food, people began to live a more settled existence. Agriculture soon spread to other parts of the world, largely replacing the hunter-gatherer lifestyle.

Later, farmers developed irrigation (watering systems) and began to use animals such as oxen to plow the soil. Crop-raising was developed around the same time independently in the Americas, where different crops such as corn and squash were grown.

This 18th-century painting shows Chinese villagers planting rice in a paddyfield. The cultivation process has changed little since rice was first domesticated thousands of years ago.

CULTURED CLONES

Cells contain all the genes needed to grow into a new organism (see **3**: 16–17). After development most animal cells switch off most of their genes. That is not the case for plants. If a developed plant cell, such as one from a carrot root, is put in nutrient-rich water, the cell will divide again and again. Eventually an entirely new plant will form. The plant produced is a clone—it is genetically identical to the plant from which the original cell was taken. This property of plant cells is called totipotency. It allows large numbers of clones of any one plant to be produced, which can be invaluable when plants are genetically modified (see **3:** 64–67) for bigger yields or to produce a certain substance.

contains plenty of starches—these chemicals are a very good source of energy for the body. They must be easy to grow from a seed or tuber, with no dormant (resting) period in their life cycle. And they must be easy to harvest; for example, to be a crop, a grass must not shed its seeds before they can be harvested.

SAVING SEEDS

Some varieties of crop plants have become very rare or extinct. These varieties have mostly been replaced by newer, more productive strains. In the long run this spells trouble for farmers.

To be healthy, a plant population needs genetic diversity (see **9**: 28–29). That helps it adapt to change, such as a new parasite. For example, if everyone grew just one type of potato, a disease could wipe out the entire crop. That happened during the Irish famine (1846–1850). Potato blight destroyed harvests, and millions of people died or had to move to other countries. Genetic diversity increases the chances of a variety having immunity against such a threat. Scientists are saving the seeds of rare varieties to conserve their genes.

Scientists store thousands of seed samples in conservation units to preserve them.

Essential staples

The most important staple crops are rice, wheat, and corn. These plants were originally short-lived plants that grew in disturbed ground. From the earliest days of agriculture people selected the

GROW YOUR OWN CLONE

Try cloning a plant by taking a cutting. Take a small twig of willow or cottonwood up to 12 inches (30cm) long. Carefully cut the twig off the main stem, and put the bottom third into water. After a week or so roots will begin to appear. Then you can plant your clone into moist potting soil and watch it grow into a new plant.

most productive individuals, saving their seeds to improve the crop for the next season.

There are several wild wheat species that have contributed to the modern crop. The bread wheat of today, for example, is the product of crossfertilization (see **3**: 61) between seven different species, as well as artificial selection of the best varieties. Over the centuries more than 17,000 different varieties of wheat have been bred for different uses, climates, or soils.

Many crop plants are planted and grown afresh each season from seeds or tubers. Fruits are different. A fruit tree can produce a good crop for many years. To increase the harvest, twigs are cut from an existing plant that produces lots of fruit. The twig is attached to the root of another tree in a process called grafting (see right). The graft grows into a new fruit tree. The new plant is genetically identical to its parent—it is a clone (see **3**: 64–67). This usually results in it sharing its parent's ability to produce fruit. Cloning is essential for a few crops, such as bananas, since they do not produce seeds.

▼ *Horticulture is the growing of fruits, vegetables, flowers, or decorative plants. Grafting is used to produce unusual plants, increase fruit or flower production, or to strengthen resistance to plant diseases.*

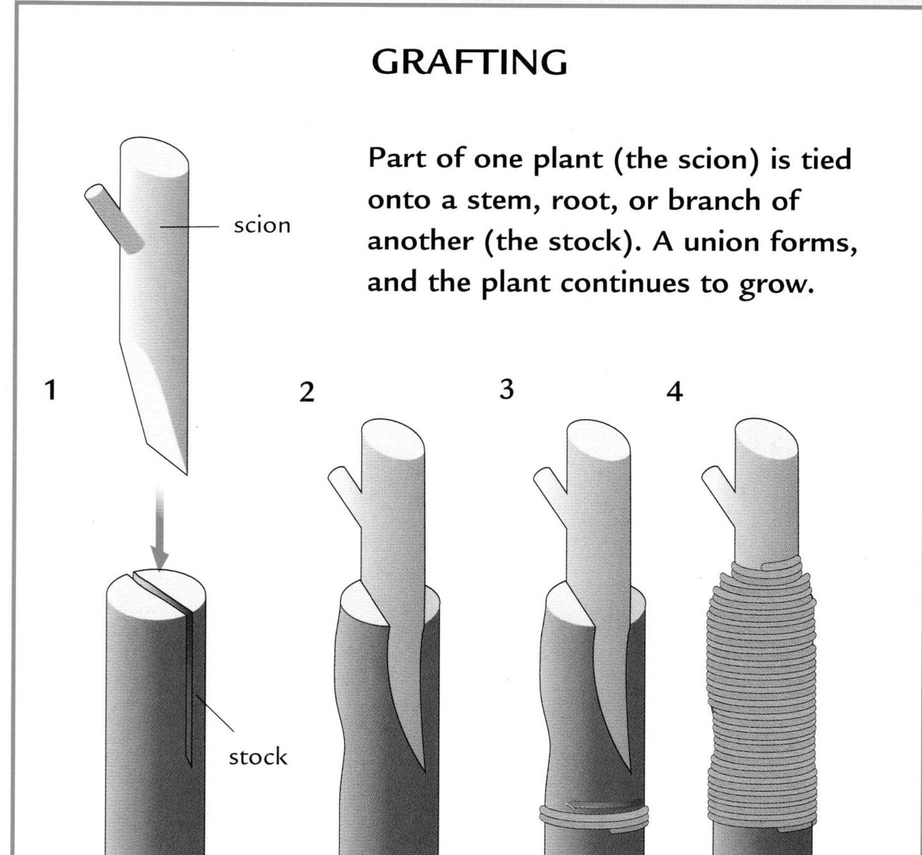

THE SEARCH FOR SPICES

There were no refrigerators in the Middle Ages. Food was preserved by salting, drying, or smoking, while fresh food soon went bad. Spices such as cloves (below) were used to cover up the taste of these bland or rancid foods. That helped food supplies last through the winter or over the course of a long voyage. The importance of using spices in food and the fact that they were traded and transported for long distances before reaching Europe meant that they were very expensive.

The search for spices and swifter routes to their sources were factors driving European exploration of the tropical world in the 15th and 16th centuries. Christopher Columbus's (1451–1506) voyage to North America was partly to try to reach the "spice islands" of southern Asia.

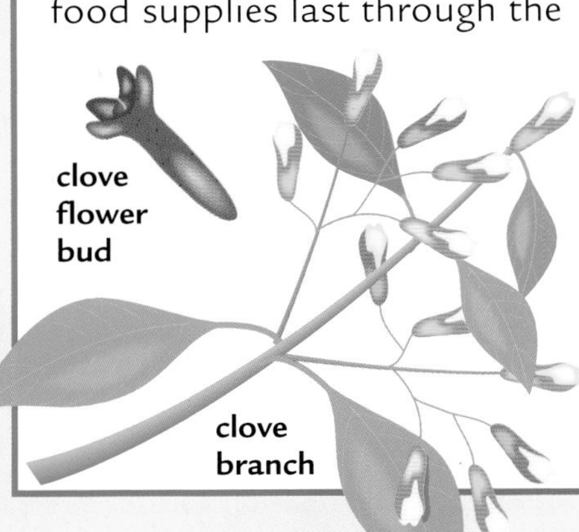

Flavor providers

People use a number of plants to give flavor, color, or a pleasant smell to food. Leaves that provide such improvements to food are called herbs. They include plants such as mint, sage, and parsley. Spices are mainly seeds or fruits of tropical plants such as black pepper and vanilla, but people also use the flower buds of cloves, the bark of cinnamon, and the rhizomes of ginger. The most expensive spice, saffron, is made of stigmas (see 34) plucked from the saffron crocus flower.

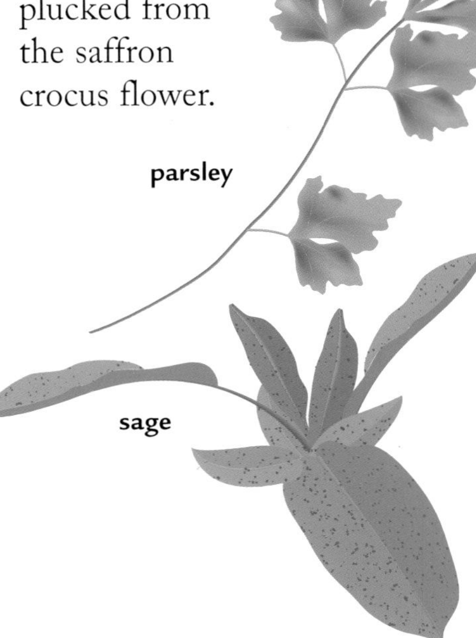

SWEET SUGAR

Have you ever wondered where the sugar in your coffee or on your breakfast cereal comes from? Like many other things we eat, sugar is a plant extract. There are two main sources of sugar: a tropical grass called sugarcane and a root crop, sugar beet.

To make sugar from beet, the roots are first washed and then reduced to shreds in a cutter. The sugar is drawn from the chopped beets by adding hot water, which dissolves the sugar. Then the sugar is removed from the water by evaporation—the water is boiled to turn it to steam, leaving the sugar behind as crystals. The crystals are boiled in water again and filtered through a very fine mesh to remove the last traces of dirt. After the water is evaporated off, the sweet sugar is ready to be packed and sent out to food manufacturers and grocery stores.

NONFOOD CROPS

Medicines

Plants have been used for thousands of years for healing, while many modern medicinal drugs contain plant extracts. Some of the more familiar drugs in the medicine cabinet came originally from plants. For example, people with headaches used to chew willow bark. It contains a drug called salicylic acid, which is an active ingredient in aspirin.

Extracts from some poisonous plants are sometimes given in small doses for healing or as an anesthetic (pain reliever). Foxglove (see below) is poisonous, but an extract from it called digitalis is used to treat heart problems.

More and more plants are being examined for their medicinal potential; extracts from the bark of Pacific yew trees help treat cancer, for example, while a tropical flowering plant, the rosy periwinkle, contains substances that fight the blood disease leukemia. The medicinal properties of very few tropical plants have been fully explored; that is one of the many reasons for conserving rich tropical rainforests.

Recreational drugs

Some people use certain plant extracts to change their mood. These mind-altering drugs can be addictive and are mostly illegal; they include marijuana, mescaline, cocaine, and opium. Opium is produced from poppies. It, and its refined forms, morphine and heroin, relieve

► *Foxgloves are extremely poisonous to eat. However, the plant is useful to people because of a chemical called digitalis, which is extracted from its dried leaves. Digitalis is used medicinally to control various heart problems.*

► *Inside a tea-processing factory in Indonesia. The tea leaves wither and are then crushed, fired, and dried.*

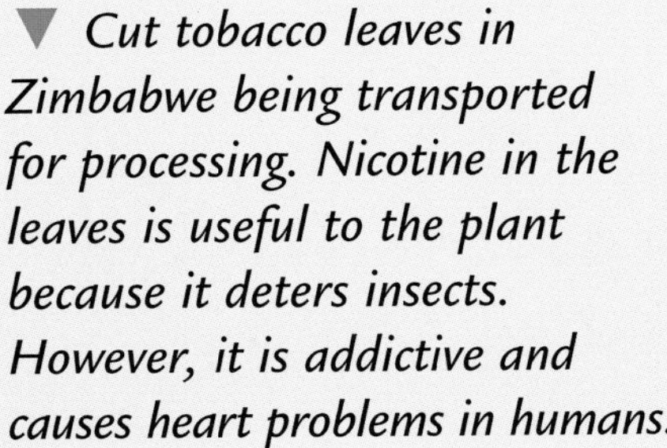

▼ *Cut tobacco leaves in Zimbabwe being transported for processing. Nicotine in the leaves is useful to the plant because it deters insects. However, it is addictive and causes heart problems in humans.*

pain, but they also affect the brain; heroin is among the most addictive of all drugs.

Some plant-derived recreational drugs are legal. They include caffeine, nicotine, and alcohol. Caffeine is a chemical present in several different plants, such as coffee and tea. Caffeine stimulates the brain, increasing alertness.

Nicotine is found in tobacco leaves. Like many of the chemicals that people use from plants, nicotine serves a defensive purpose for the plant; it is an effective deterrent to plant-eating insects. Dried tobacco leaves were smoked by native South Americans for centuries before the plants were first encountered by European explorers

▲ *Dried coffee beans alongside granules that are used to make the caffeine-containing beverage.*

in the 16th century. Smoking tobacco in cigarettes, pipes, and cigars accounts for millions of deaths each year. In addition to the highly addictive nicotine, tobacco smoke contains other chemicals that cause cancers and other diseases (see **7**: 65).

Alcohol is produced by the breakdown of sugars by yeasts (see **4**: 58) in the absence of oxygen. This process is called fermentation. Any plant that contains lots of sugar can be used to make alcohol. Barley, wheat, rye, and rice grains are all used to make beers and spirits, and grapes are fermented to produce wine. Many other plants are fermented to make drinks, such as apples for cider, potatoes for vodka, and the Mexican agave plant for tequila.

▲ *Fermented juice from the base of Mexican agave plants is used in the manufacture of tequila, a strong alcoholic drink.*

▼ *Making an instrument like a violin is a highly skilled craft. Several types of woods are used for different parts, including spruce or pine and hardwoods such as sycamore or maple.*

Wonderful wood

One of the most useful of all plant products is wood. Wood's uses range from burning for warmth and cooking to the construction of buildings and, before the 1850s, ships. Wood consists mainly of xylem cells (see 11–13). It has long been admired for its beauty in ornaments and its properties in musical instruments. Wood is strong, light, and if kept dry or treated with chemicals, resistant to decay.

An important use of wood today is in papermaking. The quality of the wood does not matter too much since it is pulped and treated during the process. The trees harvested for papermaking are usually conifers such as spruce and larch, or eucalyptus.

For ornamental furniture and sculptures certain types of trees are used; often they are tropical. Mahogany comes from a rainforest tree and polishes to a deep, glowing red. It

► *A coppice is a large area of cut-down trees. Inside it new thin stems grow densely from the remaining tree stumps. The stems are ideal for making handles for tools.*

▶ *The wood of eucalyptus trees resists decay so is useful for outdoor construction, including furniture. It is also used in papermaking.*

was frequently used for furniture when rainforest timbers were first imported to Europe in the 18th century. Musical instruments also use specific wood types; clarinets and oboes, for example, are made from African blackwood.

Wooden equipment is used in many sports, often harvested from just one or a few species of tree. The butts of pool cues are made from rosewood or ebony, while the shaft is made of ash. Cricket bats are made of willow, while baseball bats are usually made from maple.

HOT DEBATE

THE NEED FOR TREES

For thousands of years people have cut down swaths of woodland to make space for agriculture or construction. That has often led to severe environmental problems, particularly in tropical areas. Heavy rains cause tropical soils to lose their nutrients quickly, making them poor for agriculture after just a few seasons. Deforested areas in tropical areas are also prone to growing drier and drier, until they eventually become deserts where few plants can grow.

In the past whole civilizations have fallen because of environmental havoc caused by excess tree cutting. When European explorers discovered Easter Island in the Pacific, for example, the island's society was in a state of collapse. That was because almost all the trees on the island had been felled. Today Easter Island is completely treeless, and its native civilization is long gone.

Despite warnings from the past like this, global deforestation continues at an increasng rate.

Fibers

Fibers from many different plants are used to make clothing, sacking, string, and rope. Some fibers come from the stem or leaves, such as hemp and sisal. They are used for rope and sacking material. Linen is made from the flax plant and is used for clothing.

The world's most important fiber, however, is cotton. Cotton is the featherlike hairs on the seed of the cotton plant. A couple of pounds (1 kg) of cotton contain 200 million seed hairs. There are several related species of cotton native to Asia and the Americas, and the plant has been used by people for thousands of years. The plant is still grown in large quantities, although artificial fibers have replaced it for many things.

▲ *A woman harvests cotton from the plants in southern India. People use cotton fibers to make cotton garments. Cotton clothes are known for being very comfortable to wear.*

▼ *A field of flax from which linen fiber will be produced.*

Some nonwoody plants such as papyrus, which occurs in African swamps, produce fibers that can be turned into paper. Papyrus was used to make writing material by the ancient Egyptians and also to make boats and weave baskets. Scientists are now looking at ways of using hemp and even stinging nettles to make paper, since paper is a resource that is in huge demand.

▼ *Papyrus reeds growing in a swamp in Kenya. In the past these plants have been used to make paper and other writing materials.*

► *People collect latex in bowls from trunks of rubber trees. In factories the latex is used to make rubber for mats and tires.*

Other plant products

Many other everyday products come from plants. Rubber is solidified latex, a milky liquid that flows from the trunk of the tropical rubber tree (see right). Some trees produce resins that make bases for varnish, incense, and products such as the coating on paper. Other plants produce dyes like henna and woad (see 56).

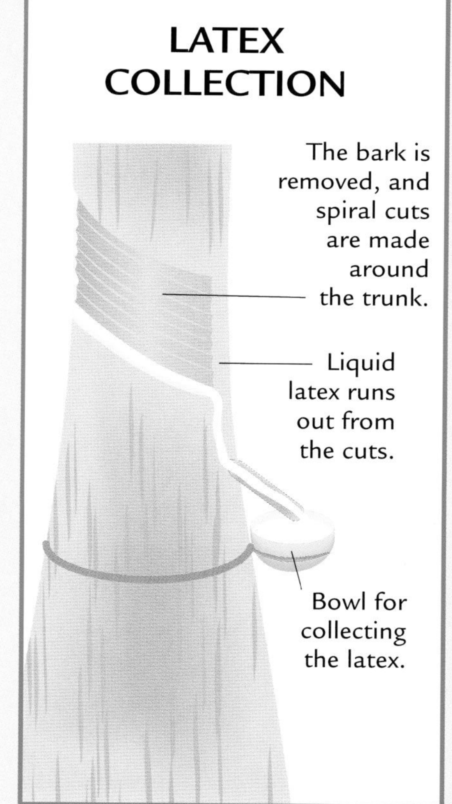

CLOSEUP

INTRODUCTIONS FROM OVERSEAS

In the past many plants in the United States were introduced, accidentally or otherwise, from overseas. Brought-in plants often do not fare well and soon die out, but sometimes a species new to an area has a major effect on native plant and animal communities.

Water hyacinth, for example, was brought in from Brazil in the late 19th century. It grows on the surface of ponds and rivers at an extraordinary rate. The plant keeps oxygen from reaching the water below, so other creatures die. Moving a ship or boat through stretches of water containing these plants becomes almost impossible since they grow very thickly. The best way to control water hyacinth is by using biological control agents (see **1**: 63) such as certain weevils (a type of beetle) and moths.

Coconut and palm oil are ingredients in soap, and many plant extracts are used in cosmetics. The bark of the Mediterranean cork oak is made into corks to stopper wine bottles. Tannins from tree bark help preserve leather and make it waterproof.

▼ *People decorate their skin with henna dye made from powder from the henna plant. Henna dye is also used for coloring hair.*

ORNAMENTAL PLANTS

Plants, especially flowers, have been grown for ornamental value in homes, parks, and backyards for centuries. Like crops, many flowers are the result of hundreds of years of plant breeding. Roses have been domesticated for a very long time; today there are thousands of varieties.

Flowers appear in many important ceremonies, like weddings and funerals, and they are often given as presents. Some ornamental plants have particular meanings; in the West roses are an expression of love, while olive leaves symbolize peace.

RARE PLANTS

Human activities have made some plants become so rare that trying to save them has

become very important. They are all part of the richness of life on Earth that we depend on. Some plants could provide vital medicines or foods in the future. Botanical gardens across the world grow rare plants, and others can be stored under cold or frozen conditions, usually as seeds (see 46). If the plants die, they can be grown afresh using the conserved seeds.

▲ *The New York Botanical Garden contains an herb garden and conservatory.*

CLOSEUP

DOUBLE FLOWERS

"Double" flowers are those with many petals, like roses. In these flowers the stamens have been replaced by petals due to natural mutations artificially selected by plant breeders.

Double flowers produce only a little or no pollen, so sexual reproduction through pollen transfer (see 35–39) is unlikely or impossible. These unusual flowers have been bred purely for ornamental value as garden plants. Like most fruit trees, their reproduction is normally from cuttings and clones.

7 Seaweeds

▲ *Red and green algae are common seaweeds. They are living side by side in a rocky seashore pool.*

Most people think of seaweeds as plants, but in fact they do not belong to the plant kingdom at all. Like plants, all seaweeds make food by photosynthesis; but they do not have true leaves, roots, or flowers, and they do not produce seeds.

The term "seaweed" is a convenient collective name for what is a very diverse group of organisms. They are all multicelled marine or brackish (semi-salty) water algae, but that is about as much as they have in common. According to the latest molecular evidence, monkeys are more closely related to mushrooms than some seaweeds are to others!

Types of seaweeds

Seaweeds fall into three major groups, the greens, the reds, and the browns. The groups are identified by characteristic pigments (colorings), but their members come in a wide variety of forms. Green seaweeds belong to the division Chlorophyta, along with several thousand other species of nonseaweed green algae. They include some of the

► *Gutweed is a fast-growing green alga that often covers upper shores forming a meadow.*

most familiar seashore species, such as gutweed and sea lettuce. They live only in shallow waters and are the least numerous of the seaweed groups, with just a few hundred species. The 3,000 or so species of brown seaweeds, also known as the Phaeophyta, include the most common and conspicuous

SEAWEED KINGDOMS

The latest molecular trees of life list about 30 kingdoms, not the standard five (see **1**: 14). Most of the 30 kingdoms contain various kinds of single-celled organisms previously in the protist or bacteria kingdoms. In this new view red and brown seaweeds are thought to be different enough from all other living organisms to rank as kingdoms in their own right, the Rhodophyta and the Phaeophyta, at the same level as animals, plants, and fungi.

SEAWEED IMPOSTORS

Not all plantlike organisms that live in the sea are seaweeds. For example, the so-called sea or eelgrasses, which form underwater meadows near shores, are flowering plants. Some of the branching weedlike organisms that grow on rocks and jetties are animals—bryozoans, sea anemones, and sponges, for example, and tiny hydroids.

▼ *The leaves of eelgrass, also called sea grass, are often 3ft (1m) long but very narrow. They are a source of food and oxygen for animals in the water.*

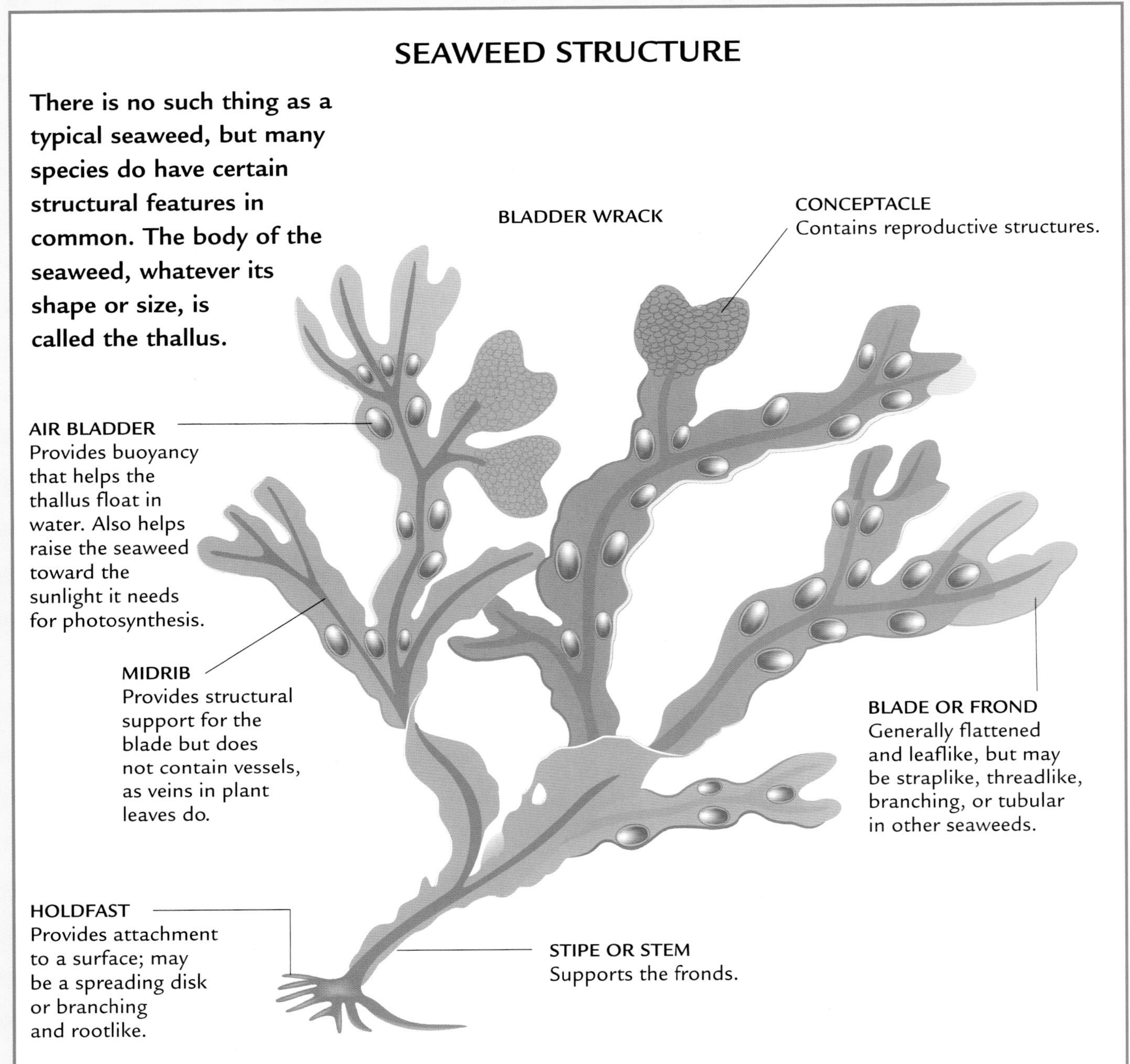

seashore species, the wracks and the kelps. Many red seaweeds are small, and others live in deeper waters. So, despite being the largest group, with more than 5,000 species, they are the least familiar.

Shapes and sizes

Seaweeds grow in an enormous variety of shapes and sizes—just as diverse as the structures of land plants. There are tall kelps with long ribbonlike fronds; encrusting red seaweeds that look more like coral or lichen; bushy, branching wracks and green algae that resemble fine hair or sheets of crumpled tissue paper. All these forms help the seaweeds survive in different kinds of marine habitat.

Seaweed habitats

Seaweeds grow in virtually all shallow marine environments, from the poles to the tropics, and in estuaries too, where river water mixes with the ocean's tide.

Seaweeds tolerate extreme environments better than most other plantlike organisms. There are species that can tolerate being frozen solid in polar ice for months at a time; others can survive prolonged periods of desiccation (drying out) while stranded high up the beach at low tide. Seaweeds living in the tidal zone are especially hardy. Their environment changes dramatically several times a

RECORD BREAKERS

The world's largest seaweeds are all kelps. They live in deep tidal water and grow very tall, so their great fronds can reach up toward the sunlight (below). Giant kelp grows more than 180 ft long (60m), taller than most trees. A giant kelp's stipes (or stems) are narrower and much more flexible than the trunks of trees because most of the kelp's weight is supported by the water.

CLOSEUP

LIVING RED STONE

Coralline red algae are red seaweeds with a difference. Instead of being soft and flexible like most other seaweeds, they are hard and brittle. That is thanks to deposits of the mineral calcium carbonate in their cell walls. Fragments of coralline red algae (right), which often look like stony branching twigs, are known as rhodoliths or maerl. In some parts of the world they build up into large beds, which are traditionally harvested for use as fertilizers and soil.

day. Immersion in cool but turbulent seawater might be followed by exposure to warm, dry air, fresh rainwater, a sharp frost, or steady warming in a tidal pool that becomes supersalty as water evaporates (turns into gas).

Making food

Like plants and other algae, seaweeds are able to manufacture their own food through the process of photosynthesis. Using energy from the sun, they combine atoms of carbon, hydrogen, and oxygen

CLOSEUP

SEAWEED SUNSCREENS

Although seaweeds need sunlight to make food by photosynthesis, it is possible to have too much of a good thing. The same ultraviolet (UV) rays in sunlight that cause sunburn in humans can damage the cells of seaweeds. To protect themselves from UV radiation, algae that live in shallow water or those exposed at low tide usually contain natural UV-screening agents such as carotenoid pigments and certain amino acids.

(all available in seawater) to make sugars such as glucose. As in plants, seaweeds contain pigments that trap the energy of sunlight. The pigments do their work inside organelles (miniorgans) called chloroplasts that occur inside seaweed cells. In most plants, and also in green seaweeds, chlorophyll is the main photosynthetic pigment.

Red and brown seaweeds also contain chlorophyll, but its color is masked by additional pigments. In red seaweeds the red and blue pigments phycoerythrin and phycocyanin combine in various quantities to produce a range of colors from pink to dark red to purple. The varied gold, brown, olive, and black hues of brown seaweeds are

A SEAWEED WEATHER STATION

Collect a strand of kelp from the beach, and hang it up outside but under cover. A front porch is ideal. Notice how the frond responds to humidity (moisture) in the air. In very dry weather it will be crisp and dry. However, some days, even before it rains, it may become soft and leathery. This is an indication that there is moisture in the air. The seaweed will detect the difference before you do. A sudden increase in humidity can signal a coming rainstorm even before the clouds gather. When the tide is out, the kelp's ability to rapidly absorb any available moisture from the air helps it survive long periods out of water.

CLOSEUP

OCEAN DRIFTERS

The Sargasso Sea is an area in the Atlantic Ocean near the Caribbean Sea. Its waters are clear, calm, and up to 23,000 feet (7km) deep. Below about 15 feet (5m) the entire sea is virtually devoid of life. But in the surface waters there is a thriving ecosystem based entirely on a special kind of floating brown seaweed called sargassum (see right). This floating forest covers a vast area and is home to all kinds of marine animals, including crustaceans, mollusks, and fish. It is also the breeding ground for millions of eels, which travel all the way from American and European rivers to the Sargasso to spawn.

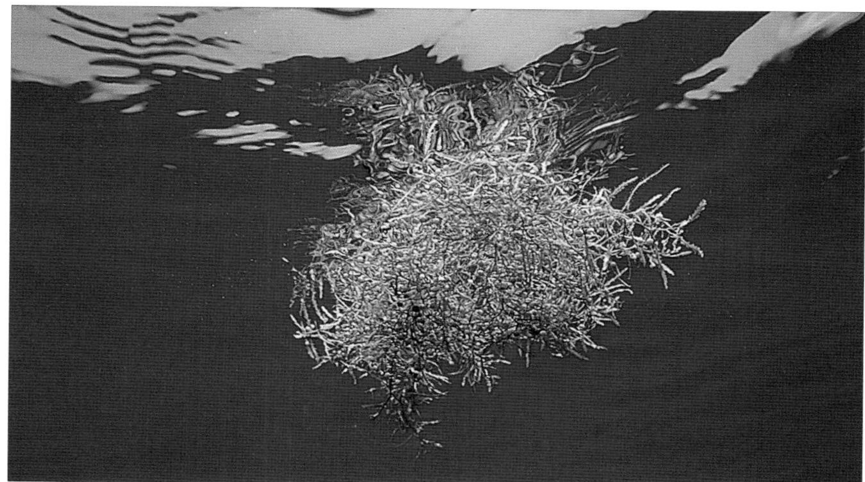

EXTRACTING PIGMENTS

Collect some brown seaweed such as kelp or wrack from the beach. Ask an adult to help you bring a beaker or pan of water to the boil. Add a strand of seaweed. After a couple of minutes the weed changes color as the brown pigments are dissolved. When all the brown pigment is gone, you should see the underlying green color of the weed.

created by a combination of green chlorophyll, yellow pigments called carotenes, golden fucoxanthin, and dark, inky-blue violaxanthin.

LIGHT AND WATER

Next time you go swimming or visit the sea, notice how the light changes as it goes through the water. Red objects look brown or black because water does not transmit red light well. Green and blue objects keep their color because green and blue light travel much better through water. Red and brown pigmented weeds absorb light from the green and blue end of the spectrum, and thus can grow in deeper water than green seaweeds.

The different colored pigments in green, red, and brown algae absorb different kinds of light from the visible spectrum. The pigments in green seaweed reflect green light and absorb red light. Red seaweeds reflect red light and absorb green light.

Seaweed in the ecosystem

Seaweeds are highly effective primary producers. That means, by converting sunlight, carbon, and water into organic (carbon-containing) compounds, they produce food for other organisms, including animals and bacteria.

The productivity of some seaweeds is staggering. In one year beds of sea palm can fix up to 30 lbs (14kg) of carbon, more than ten times as much as a comparable area of temperate grassland or tree plantation. That is three or four times as much as intensively farmed sugarcane, one of the the most productive

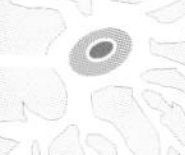

LIFE IN A KELP FOREST

Kelp beds are the marine equivalent of temperate forests. The giant seaweeds are the basis for a diverse community of organisms, including other algae, encrusting animals such as moss animals, grazers like sea urchins , sharks, turtles, crustaceans, and marine mammals including otters, whales, and dolphins.

A sea otter hunts for sea urchins around the stems and holdfasts. It uses straps of kelp as mooring lines to avoid drifting away while dozing at the surface.

Jeweled top snails hide from predatory fish and graze on small animals or the kelp itself.

Colonies of moss animals, or bryozoans, form a lacelike mat over blades of kelp.

Schooling sardines hide from larger predatory fish and diving birds.

Fish such as sheepheads and horn sharks hunt sea urchins and crabs.

A giant kelpfish uses the kelp to hide from predators. Its body is shaped like a frond of kelp and can even change color to blend into its background.

Sea urchins feast on kelp. They hide from sea otters.

Abalone and other mollusks graze on the stipes out of reach of predators of the seafloor.

A cabezon's color helps it blend in with the seafloor while waiting for prey.

Brittlestars hide from predators. At night they search for food.

Lobsters and crabs lie in wait for their prey near the stony seafloor.

of all land plants. This seems incredible until you think about the speed at which some seaweeds grow.

Bull kelp can grow up to 12 inches (30cm) in a day. Very little of this extraordinary productivity is wasted.

◀ *Many animals, such as these sea urchins, eat seaweed. Seaweeds produce vast amounts of food and thus form an essential part of undersea ecosystems.*

All kinds of animals, people included, eat seaweed. Some, such as sea snails, slugs, and sea urchins, graze on the living tissue; others make use of dead and decaying weeds. Fragments of dead seaweed drifting to the bottom of the sea are collected by a variety of detritus feeders such as brittle stars and sea anemones.

CLOSEUP

OTTERS, KELP, AND URCHINS

The kelp forests along the West Coast of the United States are home to many thousands of marine organisms. They also protect the shore from some of the force of the Pacific Ocean waves. Although the kelp grows fast, it is kept in check by grazing animals, especially sea urchins. In turn, sea urchins are eaten by sea otters (right), which controls their numbers.

Sea otters living off the California coast were almost hunted to extinction for their dense fur. As a result, the sea urchin population boomed, and the kelp forests were rapidly eaten away. Disaster was avoided by a successful campaign to protect the sea otters.

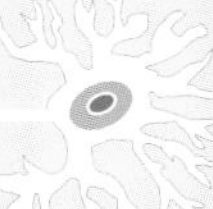

Seaweeds provide shelter as well as food for a huge range of marine animals. The floating fronds of seaweeds create a complex three-dimensional habitat that can hide large numbers of invertebrates and provide safe nursery areas for fish.

Even when the tide leaves some seaweeds high and dry on the beach, they can still be of use to animals. You only have to turn over a few fronds of seaweed on the strandline to know that underneath lurk all kinds of small animals. These vary from scuttling crabs to various mollusks and even the occasional fish. They are all taking cover or hiding in the cool, damp weed for the water to return when the tide comes in.

Seaweed reproduction

Not surprisingly for a group of organisms as diverse as seaweeds, reproductive strategies vary. Many seaweeds can reproduce asexually (without requiring the fertilization of sex cells). In its simplest form asexual reproduction usually involves the growth of a new

CLOSEUP

BEACH ZONES

Walk down any rocky beach at low tide, and the chances are you will notice several distinct zones characterized by different types of seaweed and animals (below). One particular group, the wracks, includes species that have adapted to all parts of the temperate rocky shore. At the top of the beach is the drying-resistant spiral wrack, then on the midshore bladder wrack takes over. Lower down, just above the extreme low tide mark, is saw wrack. This seaweed grows vigorously to compete with many grazing limpets and other animals but cannot withstand long periods out of water.

seaweed from part of another such as a fragment of holdfast. The new individual is genetically identical to its parent: They both have the same DNA code (see **3**: 8–15).

Sexual reproduction in seaweeds can be complicated because it often involves a phenomenon called the alternation of generations (see 41–42). Such seaweeds have two different phases in their life cycle, known as the gametophyte and the sporophyte. In some species, such as the green sea lettuce, the sporophyte and gametophyte generations look identical. In the familiar brown seaweed *Laminaria*, on the other hand, the sporophyte is large, with a simple, straplike thallus, while the gametophyte is a tiny, branching form barely visible to the naked eye.

Regardless of appearance, the most important difference between the sporophyte and gametophyte generations is in

LIFE CYCLE OF *LAMINARIA*

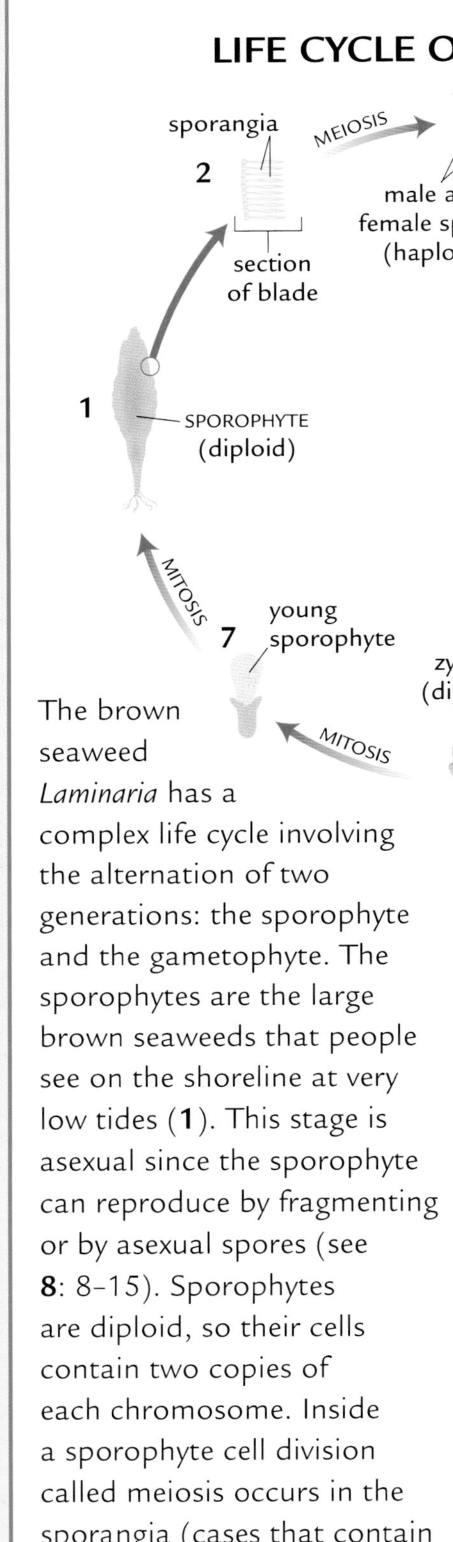

The brown seaweed *Laminaria* has a complex life cycle involving the alternation of two generations: the sporophyte and the gametophyte. The sporophytes are the large brown seaweeds that people see on the shoreline at very low tides (**1**). This stage is asexual since the sporophyte can reproduce by fragmenting or by asexual spores (see **8**: 8–15). Sporophytes are diploid, so their cells contain two copies of each chromosome. Inside a sporophyte cell division called meiosis occurs in the sporangia (cases that contain spores) (**2**). Meiosis (see **3**: 20–25) produces male and female spores (**3**), which have only one copy of each chromosome, so they are haploid. The spores are released and eventually settle on a surface. They divide by mitosis (see **3**: 16–24) to form haploid male and female gametophytes, which are almost invisible. The male gametophytes produce antheridia, each containing a single sperm (**4a**). The female gametophytes produce oogonia, each containing a single egg (**4b**). Fertilization occurs when a sperm and egg fuse (**5**). This forms a diploid zygote (**6**), which develops into a young sporophyte, again by mitosis (**7**), completing the cycle.

SEAWEED FOR GOOD HEALTH

Many seaweeds are sold as dietary supplements and health foods. They are rich in vitamins and minerals, and some have proven medicinal value. The red seaweed *Digenea simplex*, for example, is an effective treatment for parasitic worms. Other seaweeds are used as traditional remedies for rheumatism and even heart disease. Seaweed extracts are also used in many skin-care products.

their chromosomes (see **3**: 16–25). In alternating species the sporophyte generation is diploid; each cell contains two sets of chromosomes.

Seaweed as food

People have been harvesting seaweed as food for thousands of years. These days the majority of seaweeds that find their way onto dining tables are farmed (see below). Seaweed production is now a multimillion dollar industry, especially in China, Korea, and Japan, which among them produce about six million tons of seaweed each year.

THE NORI INDUSTRY

The red seaweed *Porphyra*, also known as nori, is a major food crop in Asia. In Japan it is almost a staple, making up about 10 percent of an average person's diet. Flat sheets of partially dried seaweed are used to wrap delicate sushi parcels, and dried, flaked nori is widely used to thicken and flavor soups and other dishes. Worldwide sales of nori exceed one billion dollars per year. *Porphyra* seaweed is also eaten traditionally in some parts of the British Isles. In Wales it is fried with butter and oatmeal, and served as laver bread, or *bara lawr*.

Harvesting of red seaweed in Indonesia. Dried, powdered seaweed is exported for use in the food industry.

HOT DEBATE

INVASION OF THE KILLER SEAWEED

The introduction of a tropical seaweed called *Caulerpa taxifolia* to the Mediterranean in the early 1980s was a big mistake. This species of green alga is popular in aquaria because of its bright green color, but it is now causing serious problems in the wild. It outcompetes native seaweeds and sea grasses, leaving many marine animals with nothing to eat.

The fronds of *C. taxifolia* are toxic to fish and sea urchins. The species is spreading asexually and being transported around the Mediterranean on ship anchors. Ecologists have yet to find an effective method of controlling it. There are also signs that this spreading seaweed has gained a hold in parts of Australia and off the coast of California.

Troublesome seaweeds

Usually the word *weed* is used to refer to a plant that causes a nuisance by growing where it is not wanted. This does not apply to most seaweeds, but there are a few that occasionally cause problems by fouling mooring lines and fishing nets or by making beaches and jetties slippery. Large quantities of weed cast up in storms can also create an unpleasant smell as they rot.

APPLICATIONS

ICE CREAM

Without realizing it, you probably use several products containing seaweed extracts every day. These extracts are mostly thickening agents, used in thousands of products from ice cream to paint, toothpastes, cosmetics, and even in some beers with a creamy froth. There are three main classes of thickening agent extracted from different kinds of seaweeds: carrageenans and agars come from different species of red seaweed, while alginates are a component of brown seaweeds such as kelp.

It may be hard to believe that seaweed extracts are used in the manufacture of something as tasty as ice cream!

More Information

Books

Attenborough, D. *The Private Life of Plants: A Natural History of Plant Behavior.* Princeton, NJ: Princeton University Press, 1995.

Chinery, M. *Secrets of the Rainforest: Plants and Planteaters.* New York: Crabtree, 2000.

Farndon, J. *In Touch with Nature: Flowering Plants.* San Diego, CA: Blackbirch, 2004.

Kneidel, S. *Skunk Cabbage, Sundew Plants, and Strangler Figs: And 18 More of the Strangest Plants on Earth.* New York: John Wiley & Sons, Inc., 2001.

Silverstein, A., Silverstein, V., and Silverstein Nunn, L. *Photosynthesis.* Brookfield, CO: Twenty-First Century Books, 1998.

Spilsbury, R. and Spilsbury, L. *Plant Products.* Chicago, IL: Heinemann Library, 2003.

Thomas, D. N. *Seaweeds.* Washington, DC: Smithsonian Institution Press, 2002.

Wu, N. *Beneath the Waves: Exploring the Hidden World of the Kelp Forest.* San Francisco, CA: Chronicle Books, 1999.

Websites

Agricultural Ideas for Science Fair Projects
www.ars.usda.gov/is/kids/fair/ideasframe.htm
Ideas for plant-based science projects.

Ancient Bristlecone Pine
www.sonic.net/bristlecone/intro.html
An in-depth look at Earth's oldest trees.

Brain POP
www.brainpop.com/science/seeall.weml
Click photosynthesis, seed plants, autumn leaves, food chain, land biomes, or pollination to see movies and learn about plant processes and habitats.

The Great Plant Escape
www.urbanext.uiuc.edu/gpe
Take a mystery tour to explore and understand the life cycles and structure of plants.

Internet Directory for Botany
www.botany.net/IDB
An index to botanical information available on the Internet.

Missouri Botanical Garden Photo Essays
ridgwaydb.mobot.org/mobot/photoessays
Travel with botanists to places like the Republic of Georgia and Madagascar, and learn about their flora.

NASA Earth Observatory: Plants
earthobservatory.nasa.gov/Study/PerspectivePlants
Satellite images and articles on plant cover, photosynthesis, and other botanical topics.

Plants in Motion
sunflower.bio.indiana.edu/%7Erhangart/plantmotion/earlygrowth/germination/germ.html
Plants move too! Time-lapse Quicktime movies show how plants move.

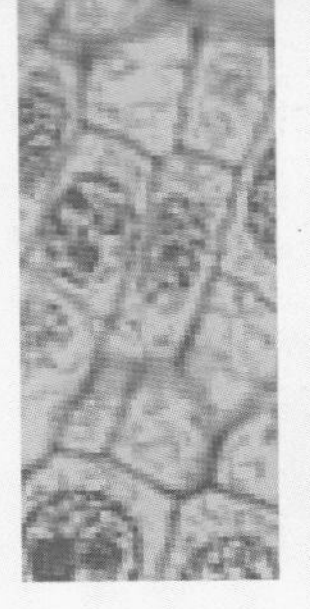

Glossary

abscission The removal by a plant of a leaf or sections of it that are infected or dying.

alga Plantlike single-celled organism.

alternation of generations Plant and seaweed life cycles made up of sexual and asexual stages that alternate.

annual Plant that germinates, grows, produces seeds, and dies in a single year.

anther Male reproductive structure that produces and releases pollen.

apical dominance When the vertical tip of a shoot grows at the expense of lateral (sideways) branches.

asexual reproduction Any type of reproduction that produces offspring without involving mating or fertilization.

auxin A plant growth hormone.

biennial Plant with a life cycle from germination to death of two years.

canopy Uppermost layer of a forest, formed by leaves and branches.

carotene A yellow photosynthetic pigment found in leaves.

carpel Female reproductive organs of a flower; consists of a stigma, style, and ovary (egg-containing structure).

cellulose Chemical that gives strength to plant cell walls.

chlorophyll Green pigment essential for photosynthesis that occurs inside chloroplasts.

chloroplast Structure in the cell inside which photosynthesis takes place.

chromosome DNA-containing structure inside the nucleus.

cuticle Waxy outer leaf layer.

deoxyribonucleic acid (DNA) Molecule that contains the genetic code for all cellular (nonvirus) organisms.

dioecious Plant with two sexes.

diploid Cell or organism that contains two sets of chromosomes.

dispersal The movement of seeds away from the adults to escape the shade of their leaves and competition for nutrients and water; seeds may disperse on the wind or in the guts or attached to the fur of animals.

epidermis Outer layer of cells of a plant. It secretes the waxy cuticle.

epiphyte Plant that grows on the trunk or branches of a larger plant.

ethylene Plant hormone that, among other effects, prompts the ripening of fruit.

fertilization The fusion of male and female sex cells.

food chain The passage of energy between organisms; a plant links to a herbivore, which in turn links to a carnivore. Energy is lost with each step.

fossil fuel Carbon-based fuel, such as oil or coal, that forms from the remains of ancient organisms.

gametophyte In plants with alternating generations the gametophyte bears sex organs and reproduces sexually.

genetically modified organism Organism with genes from another species artificially implanted into its genetic makeup.

germination When a seed begins to sprout and develop roots and shoots.

haploid A cell such as a sex cell that contains one set of chromosomes.

herbicide Chemical that kills off pest plants such as weeds.

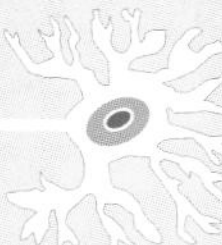

herbivore Animal that feeds on plants.

hormone Chemical messenger that regulates life processes inside an organism.

meristem Growing sections of a plant, usually near the tips of roots and shoots and at the edges of leaves.

mitochondrion Structure inside a cell that produces energy from digested food particles and oxygen.

monocarp A plant that bears fruit once before dying.

monoecious A plant that has both male and female sexual structures.

nectar Sugar-rich liquid released by flowers to tempt pollinating animals to visit.

nitrogen fixation The incorporation by soil bacteria of nitrogen in the air into nitrate compounds that plants are able to use.

parasite Organism that feeds on another but does not kill it.

perennial Plant that produces seeds over a number of growing seasons.

phloem Plant tissue that carries dissolved sugars.

photosynthesis The conversion of water and carbon dioxide into sugars in plants, using the energy of sunlight.

pollen Dustlike particles released from male reproductive structures in flowers that contain sperm.

pollinator Organism that moves pollen from one flower to another, usually in return for nectar; most pollinators are insects, but some birds and bats also pollinate flowers.

predator Animal that catches other animals for food.

scarification The scratching and wearing of a seed's surface; many seeds need to be scarified before they begin germination.

sexual reproduction Any type of reproduction that involves mating, fertilization, and the mixing of parental genes.

spore Tough structure released by fungi and some plants that can develop into a new individual asexually.

sporophyte In plants with alternating generations the sporophyte releases spores to reproduce asexually.

stamen Male reproductive organs of a flower, consisting of an anther and a filament.

staple crop One of the main food items in a particular group of people's diet.

stigma Female reproductive structure on which pollen settles and germinates.

stoma Hole on the underside of a leaf through which gas exchange takes place.

style Tube connecting stigma to ovary in the female part of a flower; pollen grows along the style to reach the eggs.

transpiration Process of water loss at the leaves of a plant.

tropism A growth response away from or toward a stimulus such as light or gravity.

turgor pressure Pressure caused by water inside a plant's vacuoles that gives the plant structural support.

vacuole Space filled with a watery liquid called sap; provides turgor pressure to the plant.

xylem Plant tissue through which water is transported.

zygote An egg fertilized by a sperm that will develop into a new organism.

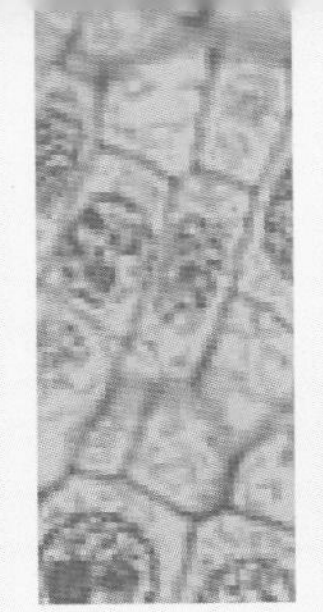

Set Index

Numbers in **bold** refer to volumes; page numbers in *italics* refer to picture captions.

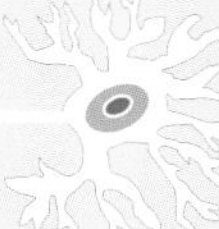